COLOUR S___

HELPING YOU
ACHIEVE SUCCESS
IN
YOUR WORK LIFE

Kara: May this be
g value in work & life

Susan

Susan Geary, PhD.
&
Anne Bulstrode, BBM FICB

Published by:
Career/LifeSkills Resources Inc.
Concord, ON L4K 2M2
www.clsr.ca

Cover Art By: Wendy Killaire - www.threedognorth.com

Photos By: Judi Douglas - www.stonephotography.ca
Thea Menagh - www.afittingimage.com

Library and Archives Canada Cataloguing in Publication

Geary, Susan, 1952-
Colour savvy : helping you achieve success in your work life / Susan Geary
& Anne Bulstrode.

Includes bibliographic references.
ISBN 978-1-894422-49-9

1. Success in business. 2. Success--Psychological aspects.
3. Color--Psychological aspects. 4. Typology (Psychology).

I. Bulstrode, Anne, 1961-   II. Title.

BF637.S8G43 2010   650.1   C2009-907540-7

Table of Contents

Acknowledgements

First and foremost we would like to thank Career/LifeSkills Resources for giving us permission to use the Personality Dimensions® terms, concepts, and ideas. We have especially appreciated Denise Hughes and Brad Whitehorn's support and encouragement through the long process of writing this book. Additionally, we would like to give special thanks Lynda McKim, principal author, and the group of dedicated facilitators who worked to develop the Personality Dimensions® model.

We would also like to thank all of the other people that help make this book a reality, those who read sections of the book and gave us insightful feedback and those who were willing to give us a view into their individual temperaments by writing the "In Our Own Words" descriptions. We would like to give special thanks (in alphabetical order) to:

Stuart Brown
Taylor Bulstrode
Carole Cameron
Scott Campbell
Christina Dawidowicz
Paul Chatterton
Galina Coffey Lewis
Andrew Geary
Jean Holm
Jennifer Madden
Ken McDonald
Ann Mossop
Sue Rawle
Allison Schiffmann
Lorrie Stobbe
Susan Sutton
Ben Waldman

Families and friends always give so much support and make some sacrifices when authors are writing. Anne would like to thank her Mum and Dad - Margaret and Guy Bulstrode for their support and ongoing encouragement throughout the process. She would also like to thank her nieces and nephew Katelyn Young, Taylor Bulstrode, and Kyle Bulstrode for their input, curiosity, great conversations, and encouragement along the way and the rest of her family and friends in Canada and around the world for their good wishes and not doubting that this book would eventually become a reality. Susan would like to thank her husband Tim Geary for his unwavering support, fresh ideas and constructive criticism, and especially for pointing to the dot of light when the end did not appear to be in sight. She would also like to thank her sons John and Andrew for their interest and encouragement and for providing an up close opportunity to learn about different temperaments.

Last, but certainly not least, we would like to thank all of our workshop participants over the last few years who gave us invaluable insight into the Temperaments from both an introverted and extraverted viewpoint and who were a driving force behind us writing this book.

Foreward

The book you are about to read could change your life.

That probably sounds like marketing hype – all froth and no real substance.

Let me assure you, it's true. *Colour Savvy* could change your life.

How can I credibly make that claim? Let me give you three reasons.

First, the framework that Anne and Susan use for helping you learn more about yourself and your career success is a powerful one. Through their writing, you are going to learn about Temperament, one of the oldest and most useful systems for understanding human nature. In fact, you are about to discover that there are *four* human natures!

From personal experience, I know the transformational power of Temperament.

Understanding Temperament has had a profound impact on my career satisfaction. Through this personality type lens, I have come to understand my core psychological needs, my innate values, and my natural talents. Gaining this awareness has allowed me to better choose work environments that meet my needs, support my values, and utilize my talents. And when those three aspects of your work life combine, it's immensely satisfying. The work I now do, I have chosen with this temperament-derived knowledge in mind. The result is a career that brings me tremendous joy and a deep sense of purpose.

An awareness of Temperament has also had a notable positive impact on my personal relationships. For example, understanding my sons' temperaments has made me a better (though far from perfect) father. The knowledge that my kids are wired differently from me, in some very fundamental ways, has helped me manage better the symptoms of the "Be Like Me" syndrome – that all too common tendency humans have for wanting to shape others into our own image. Instead of trying to turn my sons into Mini Me's, I have been able to encourage them to become fully mature versions of the type of men nature designed them to be. And they are profoundly grateful for the change in my approach to parenting!

My working relationships have also been improved significantly through my knowledge of temperament. Colleagues who used to baffle, annoy, and frustrate me have, instead, become allies and friends. I have come to see that the differences between us, while challenging at times, are actually a source of strength. Their values, perspectives, and talents supply what I often lack. This framework has also helped me "depersonalize" things that used to feel like personal attacks or affronts. Now I am better able to realize that the other person is not intentionally trying to frustrate me, hurt me, or be difficult. They are just being their temperament. Realizing this makes interactions much more effective, far less frustrating, and way more fun.

These are a few of the ways I have personally experienced the life changing power of temperament. Awaiting you, in the chapters that follow, is the knowledge that can do the same for you.

A second reason that I can legitimately declare the life altering potential of Anne and Susan's work is the practical applications that fill these pages. Both of them have used temperament for many years in their work as consultants, coaches and trainers, and their experience shines through the pages of this book. They provide vivid illustrations that bring concepts to life. They offer practical examples that make it easy to apply the ideas they are describing. And they present real life scenarios that demonstrate the validity and benefits of the principles they are discussing.

Colour Savvy is an immensely practical tool. That, too, makes it life changing.

The third reason I make this claim is the style in which Anne and Susan write. Many potentially life altering books never realize that potential – because no one reads them! After a few pages of bland prose, a ho-hum style, or fuzzy writing, people set the book aside. They may realize that it contains valuable ideas, but they can't force themselves to read the cumbersome text.

You won't have that problem with *Colour Savvy*. The authors have an engaging style that will draw you in, and hold you to the end. It's a pleasure to read this book, and that makes it so much easier to absorb its truths.

It's an honour to be asked to write the introduction to a book. In this case it's also a joy. I happily recommend *Colour Savvy* to you.

I know that if you let it, it can change your life!

Scott Campbell, President
Personalities At Work

Section 1

Introduction and Identifying Your Temperament

1

Introduction

In these challenging economic times, understanding yourself and others is a crucial skill in finding and keeping a job that you love. Our understanding of ourselves and others enables us to communicate more effectively with people, these are key competencies in the workplace. A survey conducted by the University of Pittsburgh's Katz Business School highlighted the importance of understanding and communicating with others. In their survey of over 50,000 employees, they found that communication skills (including written and oral presentations) and the ability to work with others were the main factors contributing to job success.[1]

Have you ever noticed that you really connect with some people at work and others just rub you the wrong way? With certain people, the communication flows easily and there is a high level of comfort and synergy between you, as if you have always known each other. So much so that sometimes you can finish each other's sentences. However, with others communication is more difficult. You just don't seem to be on the same wavelength, and misunderstandings are more common.

What we have just referred to is a difference in Temperament or personality. Temperament theory states that we are born with an innate drive to act in a certain way based on our core needs and values. As far back as the Greeks, different cultures have been able to identify four different Temperaments and they have been refined and built upon until the present day. David Keirsey in his book *Please Understand Me II*[2] described the four Temperaments in detail. The work of Jung, Myers and Briggs and Keirsey inspired Don Lowry, a Californian school teacher, to develop True Colors in 1979. It is a visual and highly interactive way to bring Temperament theory into the classroom.[3] Others such as Linda Berens in her book *Understanding Yourself and Others: An Introduction to Temperament*[4] and Tom Maddron in his book *Living Your Colors: Practical Wisdom for Life, Love, Work and Play*[5] have further elaborated on the four Temperaments.

In this book, we will be using the four Temperament terms identified in the Personality Dimensions®[6] tool developed by Career/LifeSkills Resources Inc. in 2003. Their work was inspired by previous theorists and represents the next level of development in implementing Temperament personality theory. The terms we will be using are Inquiring Green, Organized Gold, Authentic Blue, and Resourceful Orange.

The knowledge that you gain about the four Temperaments in this book will help you understand yourself and others more fully. By understanding yourself, you will have a better understanding of who you really are, your strengths, and unique gifts. Self-awareness can help to free you from all of the "shoulds" and "must dos" that you received as your grew up or had imposed on yourself over time. Sometimes we can be our own greatest liability, trying to make ourselves be like others that we admire or feel we should be like. With greater self-understanding, you can learn to capitalize on your own strengths and gifts and overcome your weaknesses in any work setting. It can also be comforting to know that while you are unique, there are others who share your general way of being. If you are at the stage in your life where you are seeking your first career, looking to reinvent yourself, or having to find a new job, understanding the four Temperaments will enable you to have a clearer understanding of what is important to you in a job, what career direction you want to take, and how to best present yourself to the interviewer. By understanding the Temperaments of others, you will:

- connect more positively, even with those that in the past you've had difficulty communicating with;

- appreciate the strengths and gifts that others bring to the work setting;

- let go of the tendency to try to change people to be more like yourself;

- appreciate and tolerate other's difference; adapt to different situations and people; and

- communicate effectively and build relationships with those that are quite different from you.

Completing the Questionnaire

Now it is time to find out more about yourself by determining which Temperament best fits you. To gain self-understanding, you should work with a qualified professional to reflect on your actions and behaviours and to dialogue and receive feedback. Whether it is through a one-on-one session or by attending a course, you will gain invaluable insight into yourself and others. However, completing the questionnaire will allow you to begin the self-reflection process.

When completing the questionnaire you will get the most accurate reading of your Temperament if you relax and think about how you would react when you are most comfortable. This will help you to respond from your true self, rather than how you have adapted to the world around you.

In the next couple of pages, we will ask you to respond to 10 questions. For each question, you will rate four statements. Put a four next to the statement that best reflects you, a three next to the statement that second best reflects you, and so on.

Remember to rate each question according to the following ranking:

4 = most like you

3 = second most like you

2 = third most like you

1 = least like you

1. I value:

    A. _____ Freedom

    B. _____ Relationships

    C. _____ Knowledge

    D. _____ Duty

2. I am comfortable:

    A. _____ Trouble shooting

    B. _____ Coaching

    C. _____ Critiquing

    D. _____ Planning

3. I learn best when the environment is:

    A. _____ Fun, practical, applied

    B. _____ Safe, conceptual, harmonious

    C. _____ Rational, analytical, critical

    D. _____ Specific, structured, practical

4. On the job I am:

    A. _____ Energetic, innovative, realistic

    B. _____ Conceptual, enthusiastic, supportive

    C. _____ Competent, ingenious, logical

    D. _____ Organized, responsible, dependable

5. I become stressed when there is too much:

    A. _____ Authority, boredom, lack of action

    B. _____ Conflict, lack of authority, detail

    C. _____ Injustice, incompetence, illogical thinking

    D. _____ Disorder, change, procrastination

6. In relationships, I seek:

  A. _____ Excitement, stimulation, playfulness

  B. _____ Meaning, intimacy, connection

  C. _____ Respect, intellectual stimulation, directness

  D. _____ Loyalty, responsibility, integrity

7. I enjoy:

  A. _____ Being active, applying my skills, having fun

  B. _____ Meaningful relationships, gaining insight about myself, helping others

  C. _____ Being innovative, being competent, having a logical discussion

  D. _____ Being of service to others, being recognized for the work I do, finishing a task

8. In groups, I tend to be:

  A. _____ Playful, energetic, creative

  B. _____ Inspirational, harmonizing, cooperative

  C. _____ Analytical, independent, constructive

  D. _____ Organized, committed, dependable

9. I am challenged by:

  A. _____ Taking direction, arbitrary boundaries, routine

  B. _____ Criticism, having to conform, isolation

  C. _____ Repetitive activities, lack of information, small talk

  D. _____ Risk taking, chaos, lack of control

10. When dealing with change I:

  A. _____ Adjust in the "here and now" as change happens

  B. _____ Understand how people are reacting to change and ensure that their needs are taken into account

C. _____ Think strategically and make systematic changes to achieve the vision

D. _____ Ensure that change happens effectively by implementing the specifics of the change plan

Scoring:

1. **For each question that you completed, transcribe the numbers you allocated for A,B,C,D in the appropriate space below**

2. **Then add the scores for column A, B, C and D and record the total in the space at the bottom**

Question #	A	B	C	D
SAMPLE	4	2	1	3
1				
2				
3				
4				
5				
6				
7				
8				
9				
10				
Total				

If your highest score was A it is likely that you are predominately a Resourceful Orange

If your highest score was B it is likely that you are predominately an Authentic Blue

If your highest score was C it is likely that you are predominately an Inquiring Green

If your highest score was D it is likely that you are predominately an Organized Gold

We Are All Plaid

By now, you should have a sense of your preferred Temperament. It is also likely that you have identified that you are "Plaid" – that is you are a blend of all Temperaments. While it is likely that we are most comfortable functioning from our preferred Temperament, we can and do function from all perspectives to a greater or lesser degree. Keep in mind that these Temperaments cannot and do not explain all human behaviour. They should never be used to "pigeon hole" or stereotype other people. It is also important to remember that no Temperament is better than any other is – each has its own unique talents and behaviours that contribute to the workplace.

The Four Dimensions of Temperament

The following chart will give you a brief summary of each of the four Temperaments. In subsequent chapters, we will give you detailed descriptions of each. Indeed when you read a more detailed description, you may find that you have a different preferred Temperament than you initially thought.

A Summary of the Four Temperaments	
Resourceful Orange	• Needs: freedom to act and make an impact • Has a pragmatic perspective • Gets bored quickly • Considers immediately needed actions when deciding • Focus on aesthetically and skilfully doing • Gifted tacticians, deciding the best move to make in the moment • Able to adapt and improvise • Tends to be natural negotiators
Authentic Blue	• Needs: self-actualization and relationships • Likes to develop a unique identity • Uses values such as impact on people and unity when making decisions • Effective communicators • Develops and nurtures empathic relationships • Comes into a situation with an immediate impression of what is going on with people • Tends to see the "big picture" • Likes to focus on human potential
Inquiring Green	• Needs: knowledge and competence • Uses logic when reasoning • Wants to have a rationale for everything • Focus on patterns and systems • Objective and theoretical • Develops and applies strategies • Tends to be analytical, sceptical and critiquing • Tends to be a skilled long range planner – contributing strategy, design and invention
Organized Gold	• Needs: belonging and being responsible • Believes in contribution to society and providing a service • Values the presence of order, lawfulness, security, institutions • Considers traditions and economic impact when deciding • Focus on planning, security and stability • Develops and uses regulations for efficiency • Tends to be sequential and orderly • Appreciates family and cultural traditions

Introversion/Extraversion Factor

One of the main reasons we chose to work with Personality Dimensions® and use their approach to Temperament theory, is that they add one additional dimension of personality theory. This dimension is not actually part of Temperament theory. However, it is a critical component of understanding ourselves and others – the preference for introversion or extraversion. Introversion and extraversion apply to all four Temperaments, so it is important to have an understanding of them because they play an important role in our interpersonal communications.

The Webster's Dictionary defines the words introvert and extravert as follows:

Introvert (noun) - A shy person.

Extravert (noun) - An outgoing, gregarious person.

The above definitions tend to be the way most people think of the terms introversion and extraversion. However, personality theory defines the terms somewhat differently. Jung (1923) and Myers-Briggs (1960) used the terms to describe where a person gets their energy.[7]

Extraverts tend to seek their energy from the outside world. They thrive on being around people and interacting with them, and they direct their energy outwards in the form of action. Introverts on the other hand tend to seek their energy from within themselves. They need quiet time alone to recharge their batteries and they direct their energy inwards in the form of reflection.

To discuss the differences between introversion and extraversion, we will use the example of how to prepare for and make a presentation. In the preparation stage the individual must spend time working on their own, doing research and gathering information. For an extravert this stage would be exhausting. After a day, they would need to find people to interact with to re-energize. However, the introvert would find this part of the process very energizing. It would give them the time they needed to think and reflect without interruptions from others. When it comes to the presentation, the opposite would be true. The extraverts would be in their element. They would find presenting to the audience and interacting with them to be very energizing. Again, introverts would find this part of the process draining and would tend to need some quiet time by themselves to reenergize. This isn't to say that both the extravert and the introvert aren't quite capable of doing both the preparation and the presentation itself, because they most certainly are. It is rather to explain how they would be feeling after each stage in the process and what they would have to do to regain their energy if necessary.

As we can see from the example above, introverts do their best decision-making, thinking and learning when they have the time for quiet reflection and are able to work on their own. Extraverts are at their best when they have the opportunity to interact with others, discuss their thoughts, and brainstorm new and creative ideas. Introverts may actually find that the standard brainstorming process shuts down their creative juices as it does not allow them the time they need to process internally the information before building on it or reacting to it.

When extraverts are thinking, they often process their thoughts aloud. Introverts tend to do all or most of their thought-processing internally. This can be frustrating for both extraverts and introverts when they are working with each other. The extraverts often feel the introverts are not contributing to the process, as they are not saying a lot. Actually, they are processing the information internally and they will add their ideas once they have had the chance to think them through fully. The introverts on the other hand may feel they cannot get a word in edgewise or that they are not being heard when they do say something. They can also find it frustrating because they never know if the extravert is actually planning to do what they say or whether they are just throwing out ideas. If introverts and extraverts don't understand each other, this can lead to major communication problems.

To summarize, Personality Theory defines introversion and extraversion differently from the way we commonly do in our everyday lives. Just because someone is an introvert, it does not mean that he or she is shy. Introverts can be very warm, outgoing people who can be effective at interacting with others. By the same token, extraverts are not always outgoing and gregarious and they can sometimes be quite reserved when they first meet others.

Understanding the difference between introversion and extraversion will further enhance your effectiveness in dealing with the different Temperaments. The first step in understanding the difference is to find out whether you are an introvert or extravert. Take a couple of minutes to complete the simple introversion/extraversion questionnaire that follows.

Introversion/Extraversion Questionnaire

1. For each number, put a check mark next to the statement that sounds most like you (either A or B)
2. At the bottom, add the number of As and Bs that you have checked

1.	A. I am energized by being with others		B. I am energized by time alone	
2.	A. I tend to think out loud		B. I tend to think inside my head	
3.	A. I express my thoughts and feelings		B. I keep my thoughts and feelings to myself	
4.	A. I tend to act first and then reflect		B. I tend to reflect and then act	
5.	A. I prefer problem solving by talking it through with others		B. I prefer problem solving by working it through on my own	
6.	A. Others see me as outgoing		B. Others see me as quiet	
7.	A. I have a broad circle of friends		B. I have an intimate circle of friends	
8.	A After a day working with others, I am energized		B. After a day working on my own, I am energized	
9.	A. I prefer to explore a breadth of interests		B. I prefer to explore a few interests in depth	
10.	A. I tend to project a sense of enthusiasm and energy		B. I tend to project a sense of calmness	
	Total number of As		**Total number of Bs**	

If you have, more As than Bs it is likely that you prefer extraversion.
If you have more Bs than As it is likely that you prefer introversion.

About the Rest of the Book

The rest of the book is divided into 5 more sections. They are:

- **Section 2 – Introduction to the 4 Temperaments at Work**

  These four chapters will describe how the 4 Temperaments: Inquiring Green, Resourceful Orange, Organized Gold, and Authentic Blue function in the workplace in greater detail.

- **Section 3 – The 4 Temperaments and Stress**

  Chapter 6 will focus on what causes each Temperament stress, how each Temperament reacts under stress, and how each Temperament can overcome their stress.

- **Section 4 – The ABC's of Reading and Communicating with People at Work**

  In chapter 7, we will focus on how to communicate effectively with the different Temperaments. You will learn how to read people with different Temperaments and how to effectively communicate with and influence them.

- **Section 5 – The 4 Temperaments and Finding the Right Career Fit for You**

  Chapters 8 through 11 will focus on careers. They will outline the different careers that are appealing to each Temperament and why.

- **Section 6 – The Abilities Associated with each Temperament**

  The final chapters will focus on the abilities associated with each Temperament. They will discuss how to develop expertise in each of these areas.

Section 2

Introduction and Identifying Your Temperament

In this section we will describe the needs, values, strengths, and potential challenges of each Temperament. Then a number of people have graciously provided, in their own words, a description of their Temperament. A description of each Temperament in the workplace – both in leadership and employee roles follow. Each Temperament chapter concludes by describing the Temperament traits of three superstars of that particular Temperament.

2

Inquiring Green

Needs and Values

One of the Inquiring Green's primary needs in life is to become competent and for others to see them this way.[8]   They keep working at whatever they decide to apply themselves to until they have gathered as much information and understanding about it as possible so they can feel competent. Indeed to appear incompetent or for others to call them incompetent can cause an Inquiring Green a lot of distress.

What distinguishes the Inquiring Green from the other Temperaments is their ongoing quest for knowledge. Where Authentic Blues are always striving for understanding about themselves and others, many Inquiring Greens want to acquire facts and data about the way things work as opposed to the way people work. They have a lifelong curiosity to learn new knowledge. From an early age they will ask "why" – why is the sky blue? Why does it snow? A typical example of an Inquiring Green is the little boy who takes the lawn mower motor apart and puts it back together again.

Over time, Inquiring Greens tend to develop values that will help them achieve their basic needs. High on their list of values is logical reasoning.[9]   They pride themselves on their logical thought patterns and enjoy listening to new ideas as long as they are clear and logical. If an idea is not logical, they may challenge the speaker or stop listening.

Inquiring Greens place a high value on achievement and intelligence and they are independent thinkers. They strive to achieve whatever goals they set and they impose high standards on themselves and others. For many Inquiring Greens their chosen career becomes a place where they can constantly achieve results and they can work tirelessly to be successful. Because they are independent thinkers, they do not want others telling them what to do, how to think, or which career to pursue. It is very important for an Inquiring Green to be able to make their own decisions about their chosen career and how they should go about pursuing it. When they do change jobs, it is because they want to continue to have unique or additional learning experiences.

Many Inquiring Greens value and are drawn to scientific inquiry. This meets their need to find out why phenomena are the way they are in nature and science and why things work the way they do. They enjoy the logical investigation, reasoning and universal laws behind science.

They value progress and improvement. Inquiring Greens tend not to get mired in the past or present but are oriented to the future and progression. They like to use the knowledge they gain to improve the way to do things and they can be highly effective change agents. However, this can be a source of conflict or misunderstanding with others because they may lack tact when implementing change.

Strengths

Inquiring Greens are great problem solvers and they are especially adept at dealing with complex issues – whether it is a computer, mechanical, or organizational problem. They can use their exceptional powers of concentration and vast knowledge of conceptual models and data to attack and resolve problems. They tend to be systems thinkers and like to focus on improving the way that a system works. Introverted Inquiring Greens are especially good at this because they will think through the whole issue before presenting their solution.

Because Inquiring Greens are primarily big picture, conceptual thinkers they are often effective change agents. They have the ability to look at the overall situation, understand how it works, and identify pragmatic ways to improve it.[10] Additionally, they can see the possible pitfalls and contingencies. In a variety of situations, they can frequently be visionary leaders – finding innovative ways to move ahead. They especially like being involved at the beginning of a project when they can suggest creative ideas and ways for the whole system to move forward.

They bring a healthy scepticism to everything that they are involved in, whether it is a course they are attending, a new theory, or different approach. They are often able to logically analyze the situation and find the flaw in the logic, the missing link (however, this can sometimes cause friction with others, as we don't always want our flaws highlighted). If they do find a flaw, Inquiring Greens are not scared to voice their opinions and fight for what they believe is right. They do this in a very logical manner and they don't believe in bringing emotion into this kind of reasoned argument. Equally, if someone finds a genuine flaw in their logic or theory they will generally appreciate the feedback.

Inquiring Greens enjoy new challenges as well as having the opportunity to use their intelligence and logical approach to life. They like to read, research, and gather information and can really focus when something is important to them. They bring calmness to a situation, which can be useful in stressful times.[11] They prefer to stay cool, calm and in control of themselves in crises. Even if they feel worried or excited, they will work hard to present a calm exterior. Introverted Inquiring Greens especially will demonstrate this calmness through both the body language, tone of voice and words that they use.

Anything to do with words will catch the interest of many Inquiring Greens; they are often witty and clever. They love word games, riddles, mental tricks, and repartee and tend to have a tremendous knowledge of trivia. They tend to be highly competitive in games and like to win. They enjoy any complex intellectual exercise and they like to show their mental prowess to others.

Potential Challenges

Some Inquiring Greens, especially introverts can find social situations uncomfortable.[12] As a result, others sometimes see them as cold and uncaring because they can come across as insensitive to the feelings of others. They can become impatient and show a lack of understanding towards people who bring emotional arguments or pleas into the mix. It takes them time to process emotion and feeling. They may realize they have said something hurtful after the fact. However, they may or may not clarify depending on the importance of the relationship.

Inquiring Greens can have difficulty when it comes to explaining detailed information because it makes sense to them at a big picture level and they don't realize the details are missing for others. They can't understand why it doesn't just make sense to others. In these situations, Inquiring Greens can become impatient with people and they can seem irritable and even arrogant at times.

They dislike repetitive or illogical arguments, redundancy in any form and incompetence. Unlike some of the other Temperaments who would handle this situation more tactfully, Inquiring Greens do not "suffer fools gladly" and will either withdraw or make comments that will show their impatience.

Inquiring Greens can suffer from information overload. This is especially true for Introverted Inquiring Greens if there is no opportunity for feedback or debate with others. Inquiring Greens are always acquiring new information about subjects that interest them. Because they can be prone to indecisiveness in the face of too much information this can lead to analysis paralysis and a lack of follow through on their part. They can actually end up not achieving what they set out to do. This can be very difficult for an Inquiring Green because they are highly self-critical and can suffer from feelings of inadequacy when they don't know enough, can't comprehend a situation, or don't measure up to their own high standards.

At an extreme, some Inquiring Greens can be out of touch with what is happening around them. They can focus so much on a task or a thinking process that they are oblivious to what's going. If others interrupt this process, they will be almost unable to surface – people misinterpret this as rude or ignoring them when this happens.

Inquiring Greens do not always keep to social conventions like some of the other Temperaments do. The extraverted Inquiring Green at times suffers a great deal of "foot in mouth" syndrome. They require time to process social situations – running through events afterwards. They will often realize that they may have offended others and trust that they will speak-up or debate if they have been offended, as an Inquiring Green would do. However, some of the other Temperaments may be hurt but would not be willing to speak up.

In Their Own Words

In this section, an introverted and extraverted Inquiring Green describe their Temperament in their own words:

An Introverted Inquiring Green

My needs and values:

Retaining my independence and the ability to be in charge of my own life and to make my own decisions. This has become more and more apparent as I get older too. Perhaps we become set in our ways.

It is very important that I am competent at whatever I do. It is also important to be seen as such – not so much as an "expert", but to consistently deliver great results. It's important that others see me as a talented resource, and a reliable problem solver. I tend to have a preference not to do something rather than do it poorly.

I highly value relationships with friends and loved ones that stimulate me intellectually. I also highly value the real love that comes from my friends with a preference for feeling. Wonder how they do it…

I value finishing things, and actually feel physically uncomfortable when things are not complete.

My strengths:

In areas where I have absolutely no knowledge, I'm quite prepared to accept the opinions and ideas of others who have proven expertise in the area. I list this as strength, as I suppose it is a sort of open-mindedness, albeit not without conditions!
I am extremely organized, which I value highly because it allows for efficiency. I have a process for everything. This way resources (and car keys) are always at my disposal. I despise losing anything. It makes me feel incompetent, I suppose "you dumb bunny, Carole, how could you have misplaced that…"

I'm a good problem solver, and can easily go to new ideas as well as tweaking the old ways. I don't get hung up on doing things the tried and true way.

I'm pretty darn good with words and spelling. I love word games and puzzles involving lateral thinking.
I like to understand how things work, which leads to asking lots of questions, and great conversations. I'm very good at applying what I know to a new situation particularly to solve a problem.

My potential challenges:

I generally assume that I'm cleverer than everyone else is, and therefore can discount his or her ideas initially. This is a great way to miss things, and to alienate people. It is also not logical, and quite egotistical, but it is my natural inclination. As I get older, I find I'm more able to temper this inclination, mostly because I have built up confidence in the work of others to improve or complement mine.

I can be very impatient with others, particularly when they question me, don't agree with my (logically correct) views, or just downright "don't get it". I don't have a lot of time for people who don't demonstrate any brainpower. Ironically enough, because of my preference for introversion, I have been underestimated by others in this area myself. Not openly and immediately coming out with brilliant ideas and clever comments can cause others, (ok, extraverts) to assume there's nothing going on inside my blonde head.

Another challenge is in relationships, particularly with those who have a Feeling preference, remembering to tend to this side of things. Particularly when in "action" mode, I can completely disregard the relationship side of things; it doesn't occur to me until later or when brought to my attention. I try very hard to be deliberately aware of the emotional needs of others, particularly those I value the most in my life. I tend to be more thoughtful with those I love than with the general population. This definitely slips when I'm tired.

I have never liked being "told" which can include feedback, criticism, or someone trying to "improve" my work. This does not work in favour of my own self-development.

Impact of Introversion on my Temperament:

As referenced above, when I run out of steam, and just don't have the energy to put my best face/brain/heart forward, I have been misunderstood and underestimated.

I have always been annoyed that other people (even some close friends and family) just don't "get me". For example, "if they really knew me, they'd know that I'd rather get a book for Christmas than perfume…" People probably don't really know me because I haven't let them in.

My introversion allows me to focus well and deeply on my work and on any other projects I'm involved in. I can spend days at a time writing, or doing course development without getting restless or bored. I can get a lot done in a short period of time when I choose.

I have often left the first impression with others that I'm aloof, shy, dumb, or boring. I've missed out on experiences and opportunities because I do tend to respond rather than to initiate. I'm getting better at this.

An Extraverted Inquiring Green

My needs and values:

The world through my eyes as an extraverted Inquiring Green, involves a constant quest for knowledge and to be recognized and acknowledged as having expertise in many areas of interest. Competence suggests merely able to do. As a Green, I seek far more than being able to do and mediocrity at any task or thought process is not what I strive for or value.

I tend to see everything as a problem to be solved and seek to establish a vision of the desired outcome. As a manager or a leader, I need to view others as competent in order to let go. If I see others as competent at the task at hand, I won't necessarily care about how the goal is achieved. However, I can be quite fixated on doing things my way if I am not confident in someone else's abilities or knowledge. I am very set in achieving the goal and usually quite willing to do whatever it takes to achieve that end without necessarily considering the feelings or the needs of other Temperaments.

My strengths:

My best role and forte is to act as catalyst and to be involved in the start-up or the beginning of projects, to generate possibilities, establish direction, and then allow others to follow through to universal implementation or completion. It is for this reason that I have been chosen for many pilot projects and I am a natural at establishing new concepts and services in business. I am open to change plans or direction, if the alternate route is likely to produce a logical or more desirable outcome.

I see possibilities in everything and I am unwilling to believe that something can't be done. I believe there is nothing that can't be figured out or a solution found. Often seeking others for answers and expertise in order to resolve or solve a problem, I enjoy alliances or friendships with others who have expertise or knowledge that I can learn from for myself or draw upon if required in the future.

I actually have taken things apart physically to know how they work (computers, clocks, etc.). I also approach problems, circumstances, and situations by taking them apart and seeking new or existing concepts, models or systems for better understanding and application.

I have incredibly high standards and set them for myself with the impact of challenging others to produce their best work. In many team settings, I compete with myself and my past performance, and may have the impact of raising the bar for others to achieve things they never believed they could do.

I tend to move from one thing to another to learn or apply new approaches to the way things are done. The need to be intellectually challenged is strong and sometimes follow through is lacking when boredom or mastery is already present.

I have a unique ability to tap into my subconscious when asleep and awake in the morning with an answer to problems that may have eluded me in my waking hours. This ability can break the stalemate of paralysis through analysis. This may take practise and is a skill that I have discussed with other Greens. This ability can be especially significant when I have generated many ideas and cannot process to a conclusion or find the best solution (paralysis through analysis). I can also wake knowing how to do something that eluded me the day before e.g. tying a bow tie, a dance step or solve a problem. (I believe that everyone has this ability but may be more pronounced or prevalent in Inquiring Greens)

My potential challenges:

Aware of the characteristics of my own Temperament, I may want to include the feelings of others in a decision and yet will still go with logic because I view the logical decision as the inevitable choice. Delaying a decision or a course of action is therefore viewed as procrastination and not logical. Delivering bad news or honesty in a relationship may be better served if, as an extraverted Inquiring Green, I gave more consideration to timing.

As an extraverted Inquiring Green, I will often not see the hurt caused until after the fact or until I've had a chance to process and think about social situations. I also may or may not seek to clarify any misunderstandings. This will depend on the importance of the relationship. The difficulty being that I don't always view work relationships as relationships that require the same caretaking tendencies as personal relationships. This can cause problems in today's team environments.

Getting stuck and being unable to brainstorm can be the result without external stimulation, either through conversation or debate or by not connecting with the external world. This is usually when paralysis through analysis happens for me as an extraverted Inquiring Green. I am not always good at following processes if I think I know a better way or if the existing process involves steps that aren't logical to me. My motto might be, "It is better to beg forgiveness than to ask permission." I will often invent or create my own approach to a goal or outcome to remain stimulated by a redundant or mundane routine or if goals are unclear from the outset.

I may not always express my emotions or feelings with people that I don't know well and my feelings can be hurt if others view me as insensitive, believing that nothing can hurt my feelings. I need time to process, very much like computers of the past, updating at night. Still waters run deep and I am likely to retreat or withdraw if being viewed as incompetent with feelings and emotions.

Under stress, I can become scattered, forgetful; lose all sense of order and process from an importance standpoint. This can result in focusing on unimportant details or getting stuck on an issue that is not a priority in order to gain a sense of competence or control in a situation.

Impact of Extraversion on my Temperament:

As an extraverted Inquiring Green, I think out loud and may say things that I don't believe in or adhere to myself. I like playing devil's advocate because it is stimulating for me. After all, I'm just thinking out loud. I like to debate opposing views to come to the best solution or just for the sake of expressing different ways of seeing things. I don't take my own thinking out loud too seriously, and find it hard to understand why others may hold me to what I've said while thinking out loud. The best outcome or solution is what counts, and not what was said previously. It's all part of a forward moving and an ongoing process for me.

I definitely suffer from "foot in mouth" extraversion with a Green focus on knowledge and competence instead of feelings and relationships. Things fly out of my mouth, without any apparent thought to their impact. There is no time to exercise any judgement or even to self-edit. In the same way that I sometimes know the answers to riddles, puzzles and problems, intuitively and instantly, I will say things with the same abandon. Counting to twenty before I speak has helped with feedback and the understanding of others.

The extraversion piece may not necessarily involve connecting with people to become energized and may involve just connecting with the external world. This may involve talking to myself to hear my own thought processes or even just being outside, in nature or around people. When working alone, I may need external noise like a radio or television to remain energized and will prefer quiet if deep concentration or problem solving is involved.

Inquiring Greens at Work

The Inquiring Green Leader

Inquiring Greens can be visionary, strategic leaders[13]. They use their visionary abilities to determine new ways for their organization, department, or team to move forward. They use logical reasoning and systematic thinking to analyze potential possibilities and pitfalls and determine the best direction. Once they have created their vision, they develop meaningful objectives for their followers to implement. Their pragmatic nature will ensure that they constantly scan the environment to guarantee that results are being achieved. They will then revise their direction as necessary in order to achieve their vision. Ideally, they surround themselves with competent employees who are as equally capable and hard working as they are.

As leaders, Inquiring Greens are highly effective change agents and innovators who are often open to new possibilities. Traditions or the past do not mire them down. When implementing change in organizations, they will scrutinize structure, roles, and processes to find the flaws and determine what needs to be changed. Using a systematic, rational approach, they will design and implement new processes. Inquiring Greens are in their element when they can invent new ways of doing things. Because of their scientific and technological bent, they are firm supporters of research and development activities within organizations.

They analyze situations in a logical manner before they act, gathering sufficient facts and data to ensure that they understand the whole system. They do not take new information at face value – rather they critique and verify information before accepting it. As conceptual thinkers, they relate information to underlying theories and philosophies from a wide range of sources. They use diagrams, flow charts, maps and other systematic tools to understand situations and explain them to others.

By bringing a cool-headedness and calmness to situations, Inquiring Greens can be very effective in stressful, rapidly changing times. They will work hard to remain outwardly calm even if they don't feel that way. This can instill confidence in their employees and enable them to problem solve rather than panic. Because they tend to critically analyze systems and information, they will frequently locate and point out flaws to their employees or associates. However, they will do this in a calm, rational manner and are quite comfortable debating issues in a reasoned way.

Inquiring Greens can be effective coaches and teachers because they want to contribute to the competence and knowledge level of their employees and the organization as a whole. They teach from an expert base imparting their knowledge, principles, and techniques to their employees. They will bring in outside experts, provide readings, or technological tools to help their followers learn. However, they can become quite impatient if the people they are teaching or coaching don't get it the first time. Having to repeat themselves is frustrating to them because they detest redundancy. Their expectation is that their followers will pay attention and get it right the first time by making use of the information they have been given.

While their strengths are in developing a vision and strategy, they may have difficulties in communicating them clearly. Sometimes they can confuse their listeners by being too abstract or overly technical. At other times, because of their distaste for redundancy they may only state their message once. This does not always give the other Temperaments sufficient time to understand the message fully.

Some Inquiring Green leaders are not socially sensitive towards others. They may not recognize the importance of positive feedback or recognition because they themselves may feel uncomfortable receiving it or feel they don't need it. This may be especially hard on the Authentic Blues and Organized Golds because they flourish when they receive positive recognition. Additionally, Inquiring Greens may not tune in to the positive or negative feelings of others. Their employees may see them as distant or aloof and avoid approaching them with work or non-work related issues. In times of change, Inquiring Green leaders can become vulnerable if they do not understand the feelings of others because unhappy employees may sabotage change efforts.

The perfectionist tendencies of Inquiring Greens can make it difficult to work for them. They can become irritated with employees who make mistakes or who ask them to repeat what they have already said. In the name of improvement, their natural tendency is to look for the "flaws" in everything and some employees can find constant critiquing demoralizing.

Tips for Working for an Inquiring Green Leader

- Present your arguments in a logical manner
- Be open to new ideas
- Be proactive
- Show confidence
- Be willing to debate ideas
- Be open to feedback and critiquing
- Be a problem solver, come to the table with a solution
- Be innovative
- Show initiative
- Present ideas at the conceptual level
- Keep your cool, don't get flustered
- Be future focused, don't dwell on the way it has always done it
- Don't get offended by their bluntness
- Don't make small talk
- Don't be redundant

The Inquiring Green Employee

Inquiring Greens really live up to their name when it comes to the work place. They are motivated by their curiosity and they need to know why they are doing what they are doing and how things work.[14] Whether it is something mechanical, a problem that needs to be solved, or a process or structure that needs to be designed they are the person for the job. An Inquiring Green is motivated when they can put their curiosity to good use. They need the freedom to figure things out for themselves and then to act on what they have discovered. Given this freedom, they can be major contributors to any workplace.

Data and information are what it is all about for Inquiring Greens. To them knowledge is power and they have an ongoing need to learn new information. They are in their element when gathering data and information, analyzing it, strategizing and using it to create a new design, process, or structure. The early stage of a project is when they enjoy becoming involved and where they excel because they can make the best use of their skills and creativity. However, once this stage is complete they are often ready to move on. Some are not always interested in follow through or implementing what they have created.

Inquiring Greens are future focused and like to think in an abstract manner and approach things from an intellectual point of view. They are not likely to accept the explanation "this is the way we have always done it". They want to understand the way things work, why they are doing what they are doing and maybe look for ways to improve things. They are natural systems thinkers who really enjoy analyzing complex patterns. Because of this they can be very instrumental in times of change and uncertainty. They can look at a situation from a strategic point of view and come up with inventive ways to overcome obstacles and develop innovative solutions.

When decision-making, they don't base their decisions on sentiment or tradition – it is all about the facts and just the facts. They pride themselves on not being taken in by the emotions of the situation. They tend to be rational, logical, and sceptical and are not willing to settle for the easy answer. They will critically analyze the data and look at a situation from all sides before making a final decision. Actually, the facts and trying to make sure they have all the information can sometimes bog them down.

The Inquiring Green's wit can tend to be on the dry side and at times they can come across as being sarcastic or even cold. They do not enjoy small talk, sloppy thinking, or redundancy. This could lead to some team problems if the other team members don't understand this is just the way the Inquiring Greens are and they don't mean to offend anyone. They enjoy a good discussion and debate with a cool, calm, and collected demeanour. Unfortunately, because of their powerful debating abilities and their lack of sensitivity to the emotions of others they can be perceived as argumentative at times. If the discussion becomes emotionally charged, Inquiring Greens can become very uncomfortable. If they do become angry or upset their emotions can bubble over and they may feel the need to temporarily remove themselves from the situation. This will give them time to regain their equilibrium and refocus from a logical point of view.

Many Inquiring Greens are not good at tooting their own horn. However, they do like it when others recognize them for their competence. It is important to them to put their abilities to good use. This is a key factor when it comes to managing an Inquiring Green. They do their best work when allowed to make use of their analytical skills, strategic thinking, and creative abilities. They don't tend to do well in positions where they have to follow a set routine, do a lot of repetitive work, or where their work requires a lot of follow through.

Good career choices for Inquiring Greens are those that allow them to put their analytical skills, intelligence, and ingenuity to good use. For example, research and development is an ideal career for some Inquiring Greens. They are best to stay away from careers that require them to deal with the emotions of others or to do repetitive or highly detailed tasks.

Tips for Managing an Inquiring Green Employee

- Explain the "why" behind what you are asking them to do

- Allow them leeway in how to do the job

- Give them opportunities to problem solve

- Don't give them highly detailed or repetitive tasks

- Allow them opportunities to be innovative

- Don't micromanage

- Expect them to challenge the status quo

- Don't be put off by their cool exterior

- Give them the opportunity to learn and take on new tasks

- Present your ideas to them in a logical manner

- Don't become emotional with them

- Don't explain the same thing over and over again

- Make use of their analytical skills

- Recognize their competence

- Help them to understand their impact on others

- Don't try to engage them in small talk

- Allow them to be curious

Inquiring Green Superstars

Martin Luther King

Martin Luther King, an African American Baptist Minister, is renowned as an activist leader who was pivotal in moving the civil rights movement ahead in the United States. He was a visionary leader who organized and led marches for basic civil rights, such as the right to vote. An intellectual with a tremendous thirst for knowledge, he received a Ph.D. in theology from Boston University. He decided that the Ministry could be both intellectually challenging and inspiring from an emotional point of view.[15] Ghandi's concept of non-violent resistance also inspired him and he dedicated his life to non-violent activism.

He was highly innovative in his use of non-violent activism because he strategically chose locations, times, and methods of protest that created maximum impact. Newspapers and television covered these protests and this generated a lot of public sympathy for the civil rights movement. Martin Luther King was a brilliant orator, who used his intellect, his conceptual and strategic focus, and his ability with words and stories to inspire his listeners. His "I Have a Dream" speech is regarded as one of the finest speeches even written and delivered. Through much hardship, poverty and imprisonment King never lost sight of his vision of civil rights for all. He was awarded the Nobel Peace Prize in 1964.[16]

Pierre Elliot Trudeau

Pierre Trudeau was a charismatic leader who dominated Canadian politics from the late 1960s until the mid-1980s. He was the Prime Minister of Canada from 1968 to 1979 and from 1980 to 1984.[17] Highly educated, he first earned a law degree in 1943 at the Université du Montréal and then continued his studies outside of Canada with a master's degree in political economy from Harvard University's Graduate School of Public Administration. In 1947 he studied at the Institue d'études politiques de Paris in France, and finished his studies at the London School of Economics working towards a doctorate. However, he never finished his thesis.

From his early career in the late 1940s until his death on September 28th 2000, many considered him an intellectual. He had a vision for Canada to become a "Just Society". He vehemently defended universal health care and regional development as two ways of achieving his vision and making Canada a better place. In his first years as Prime Minister he implemented official bilingualism one of his long time goals. This legislation made it mandatory to offer all Federal services in both French and English. He was also instrumental in reforming the Canadian Constitution with the *Constitution Act*, 1982.

Like many Inquiring Greens, he was not scared to voice his opinions and fight for what he believed in. Even after retiring from politics on June 30th 1982, he remained influential, writing and speaking out against both the Meech Lake and Charlottetown Accord's proposals to amend the Canadian Constitution. He argued that they would weaken federalism and the Canadian Charter of Rights and Freedoms if they were to pass. Many consider his opposition a critical factor in why both proposals were defeated.

He remained active in international affairs, visiting foreign leaders and participating in international associations such as the Club of Rome right up until his death on September 28th 2000.

Woody Allen

Another famous Inquiring Green, Woody Allen is a renowned film director, writer, and actor whose films reflect his own creative vision and style. He personally writes and directs his movies and has acted in many of them. As an intellectual, he draws heavily on literature, psychology, philosophy, religion, art, and love for the creative ideas for his movies.[18]

An independent thinker, he soon realized that he wanted complete control when making films. This stemmed from his earlier experiences on films such as "What's New Pussycat?", "Casino Royal" where meddling producers, stars, and directors could significantly change the direction of a film.

He has an impressive body of work in several creative areas. As a film maker he has won three Academy Awards and been nominated on many occasions for his work as a screen writer, director, and actor. He is a successful stand-up comedian – portraying an intellectual, neurotic, anxiety-ridden persona. As a musician, he is an accomplished jazz clarinettist, who has performed publicly on a number of occasions. Last, but certainly not least, he is an author who has written plays and has had essays and short stories published in magazines like the *New Yorker.*

3

Resourceful Orange

Needs and Values

Freedom is of ultimate importance to Resourceful Oranges. They want to have the option to make immediate decisions as the need arises. They want the ability to express themselves in whatever way they choose – whether in the arts, music, business, or adventure. In their work, they want control over how they accomplish their job. Without this kind of freedom Resourceful Oranges can feel constrained and boxed in, which may result in them letting others down.

Excitement and action are highly valued by Resourceful Oranges. From the time that they are little they hate to sit still and listen for too long and they are always looking for something exciting to do (which can often get them into trouble, especially in school!). They like to live in their five senses (sight, sound, touch, taste, and sense of smell) as much as possible and have new sensations and experiences. They love to be spontaneous and go with their impulses because that is when they truly feel alive.

For them variety is the spice of life. They love change and unpredictability in both their personal and professional life. For example, they may enjoy changing residences, vacation spots, restaurants, recreational activities, or routines. Most Resourceful Oranges dislike being bored and they do whatever they can to ensure that they are not in that situation.

Resourceful Oranges take pride in becoming proficient and recognized in their chosen endeavour. Their goal is to become people who are capable of a perfect or near perfect performance. A Resourceful Orange's chosen endeavour can range from music, acting, arts and crafts, sports, cooking, business, politics and many more. Whatever they choose, they will aspire to be the best.

Resourceful Oranges yearn to make an impact on society.[19] They want to leave their mark and if they can't do it in a positive way, then they will do it by standing out from the crowd and shocking or defying society. Because of their desire to have an impact, they often enjoy careers in politics where they can use their tactical ability, flexibility, and ability to perform under pressure to achieve results. The entertainment and arts worlds where they can use their creativeness and ingenuity to have an impact on society is a draw for some. For others, activities that involve working with tools draw them. Some Resourceful Oranges just have an innate sense of how mechanical things work and can make them work well.

They enjoy being challenged and tend to take risks.[20] Sometimes, they will do something just to prove they can – not just to prove it to others but more importantly to prove it to themselves. For example, when asked, "why did you climb that mountain" a Resourceful Orange's answer might be "because it was there". They don't want easy tasks, as these quickly bore them. A challenge gets the Resourceful Orange's adrenalin going and keeps them on their toes – whether at work or at play. Quite frequently, they find professions or sports that require them to take physical risks such as off shore oil drilling, high rise construction, mountain climbing, sky diving, surfing or white water rafting is very attractive.

Resourceful Oranges believe in enjoying themselves and having a good time. Their motto is seize the day – life is to be enjoyed.

Strengths

Of all the Temperaments, Resourceful Oranges are the most adaptable. Because of their ability to flex in the moment and respond to new circumstances others often refer to them chameleons. They function optimally when they need to work to tight deadlines or juggle multiple priorities. They come into their own in crisis situations. When things get tough, they don't panic, – they jump into action, identify what to do, and respond skillfully to deal with the emergency. This is why they often enjoy careers such as fire fighting or the police force where they constantly need to respond appropriately in the moment.

Resourceful Oranges take pride in being skilful performers. When they are interested in developing a skill or behaviour, they will work tirelessly and use considerable time, energy, and resources to perfect their ability. Indeed, some Resourceful Oranges will dedicate themselves to perfecting their technique, whether a sales pitch, a software tool, or a presentation technique. However, they don't tend to learn by reading books or being given instructions, their learning style is much more hands on. They learn by being shown how to do something and then doing it. Resourceful Oranges truly believe that practice makes perfect. Many relish performing and do it with grace and style. While other types can suffer from performance anxiety, Resourceful Oranges can actually perform better under pressure.

They can be masterful negotiators and promoters. They have the ability to charm others and win their confidence. They have a natural cynicism about people, which helps them as negotiators because they are always thinking, "What's the other person looking to get from me?" They are highly attuned to people's body language and tone of voice and are able to "read" them easily. They are skilled at using whatever they have at hand in the moment and taking advantage of it when they negotiate. They make use of these abilities to obtain the best deal they can. While others might find negotiations stressful, Resourceful Oranges are energized and excited by them. Extraverted Resourceful Oranges are often excellent promoters. They can be highly persuasive and quick on their feet and tend to win people over easily.

Resourceful Oranges are tactically gifted. They use their senses to scan their environment, assess what is happening, look for opportunities, and choose the most successful course of action. They are interested in using whatever tools they have at hand to achieve their goal. For example, if a Resourceful Orange was hanging a picture and did not have a hammer available they could just as easily make use of the heel of a shoe or a paper weight to hammer in the nail. They have a natural affinity for instruments, machines, and equipment of all kinds because it extends their ability to perform. If they have a BlackBerry®, they will use it to its maximum advantage. They will learn how to use all of its functions by playing with it and figuring out everything it can do and how it all works rather than by reading the instruction manual.

They are often effective problem solvers and trouble shooters. Their talent generally lies in their ability to focus on practical issues rather than those in the conceptual realm. Resourceful Oranges are realistic and focus on what works best. Because of their ability to think creatively, they often come up with a variety of potential solutions to the problem at hand, working best when they are given a project or tool and allowed the freedom to change it or rework it to make it work better. Because they tend to be decisive, they prefer to act quickly to resolve a situation rather than spending time thinking or talking about the problem.

Resourceful Oranges can make a great contribution to work teams. They are generous and fun loving team participants. They will work energetically and enthusiastically to achieve the team goal when they buy into it. They are very hard workers and will always put in that extra bit of effort to get the job done. Resourceful Oranges, especially extroverted ones will be high energy, active team members.

Unlike the other Temperaments, Resourceful Oranges generally take a light-hearted attitude towards life. The other Temperaments tend to benefit from this sense of fun and playfulness. Many extraverted Resourceful Oranges enjoy telling jokes, playing pranks, and finding ways to make other people laugh. Wherever possible, they like to turn their work into something fun and enjoyable and bring a welcome sense of levity to any business environment. They are the world's optimists and usually see the cup as half full rather than half empty.

Potential Challenges

Resources Oranges are often the life of the party. They need freedom, and can become bored easily, none of which are bad things. However, they are often misunderstood and others sometimes think they are immature, rambunctious, noisy, disordered, careless, hyperactive, or lazy by the other Temperaments. Most Resourceful Oranges don't let other's perceptions bother them and live their lives in a way that works for them and allows them to be productive members of society.

However, some Resourceful Oranges are not able to fit in as well as others and can become unhappy, unfulfilled, and start to buck the system. When they are young, they may demonstrate their boredom by acting out or lying. In extreme cases, some may drop out of school because it bores them or they may run away from home because they don't like living within the rules. Because of their need for freedom, they may see it as justified when they break the rules, or even the law. Resourceful Oranges are also natural risk-takers and adventurers. Always ready to try something new, they especially enjoy physical activity. Extreme sports, such as hang-gliding and bungee jumping often draw them because they enjoy the adrenaline rush. The problem is once they have done these activities they can become bored with them. The saying "Been there, done that, got the T-shirt" often sums up how a Resourceful Orange feels. To keep things interesting they want to either move on to something new or take more risks within the same sport. Consequently, some can get themselves into potentially dangerous situations.[21]

Many Resourceful Oranges get an adrenaline rush or a "buzz" out of taking risks. In some extreme cases, if they are not able to get this buzz naturally they may try to find it in other ways such as taking stimulants like energy drinks and caffeine. This can heighten their excitement and remove any fear or anxiety they may be feeling. It is important that Resourceful Oranges find productive outlets for their energy and enthusiasm; otherwise, they can end up getting themselves in to trouble.[21]

In Their Own Words

In this section, an introverted and extraverted Resourceful Orange describe their Temperament in their own words:

An Introverted Resourceful Orange

My needs and values:

I like to have freedom – to do the things that I want and go where I want. As a person just going into the workforce, I am hoping that I can find a job that allows me the freedom to get the job done in my own way without too much structure. I greatly struggle with people telling me what to do, especially if I do not feel like they are in a position to do so.

It is very important to me that my peers and social groups respect me. Because of this, I can hold back in big social groups because if I say things or contribute in a large way, I have put forth something that can be judged or criticized. If I do not value the people that might judge me, I do not care about their opinions. However, if it is an area in which I would like to excel and I respect the people involved then I care deeply about what they think of my opinions. In a nutshell, my needs and values are to be respected by the people I care about and colleagues I look up to.

My strengths:

As a Resourceful Orange, I am very capable of reading different people's emotions and it means that I can be very successful at adapting to other types of personalities and knowing how to interact effectively with people. This also allows me to be able to read what people want and it can be very helpful in settings such as job interviews.

I have found that I can apply myself effectively to many different tasks and situations. While I was a university student I worked successfully as a carpenter, a counsellor for foreign students, and a researcher.

I also like working with and using tools. As a carpenter in my summer holidays, I bought the best tools that I could and kept working with them until I was proficient. In my current position as a researcher I have enjoyed learning how to use tools such as GPS, GIS and radio telemetry and I get great satisfaction in everything I do. I don't enjoy asking for help.

I have found that I can problem solve – especially in difficult or emergency situations. In these situations, I can generally come up with a variety of potential solutions to the problem at hand and quickly implement them.

Potential Challenges

Because I like to live in the moment and keep my options open in case something interesting comes up, others may perceive that I do not always follow through because I may change my plans at the last moment. Additionally, I find it frustrating working with people who are very organized, which is the opposite of my carefree style. I can also get bored and stressed out if I have to do too many routine tasks and I would hate to do a desk job. I would not thrive in an environment where there is a lot of routine paper work or strict time lines and generally, I am very poor at making deadlines on time.

Impact of Introversion on my Temperament

Being an introvert can be very challenging. It often seems like we live in an extrovert's world. This is a challenge when you know you are going to be in large social settings that are unavoidable. But, when it is a decision that has to be made, I will choose to go for a social setting that is more intimate than, say, a crowded bar. This seems to be the best way to deal with my introversion because I will never be able to compete with those extroverts so I have to create opportunities where my personality can come through to interesting people. In addition, in many cases it is more likely that I will not become friends with someone until I have a long period of time for my personality to come through.

An Extraverted Resourceful Orange

My needs and values:

One of my needs as a Resourceful Orange is to take risks and I have certainly taken my fair share – especially when it comes to sports. However, I would like to think that I take calculated risks. Would I get on a Big Dipper or Ferris Wheel at the "EX" – the answer is definitely a big NO. Would I change a head sail on a sail boat in the middle of a long distance race in rough seas at two in the morning – the answer is yes and I have done it. In fact, I have done quite a lot that would be considered dangerous, but my underlying comfort level is that there must be an element of my being in control. The Big Dipper – where I have no control whatsoever, scares me to death. I suppose one could argue that I don't have control when I am in an aircraft but there are times when you put your life in the hands of someone more capable than you are. The pilot has the skills and his life is at stake as well as my own. I think I can trust him!!

Life should be fun and enjoyable. You should not take it too seriously. I have been lucky in that I have always worked in an environment with fun people who didn't take themselves too seriously and were always willing to see the lighter side of life. My goal outside of work has been to enjoy myself. I have always had a very active social life and my wife and I have entertained people frequently in our own home. I have also had a good time in the sports activities that I have engaged in. Currently, I enjoy skiing and golf and when I was younger much more adventurous activities.

My strengths and potential challenges:

In my business life I have always been involved in the sales and service field. If I think about it my Resourceful Orange status first showed itself in my very first job interview at the grand age of seventeen and three quarters. I applied for a job as an office trainee only to immediately be offered a role that would expose me right away to the company's clients and markets – a much more exciting role. I continued in this capacity throughout my career, the only difference being that as I got older the clients became more important and the stakes much higher. I grew to become a senior executive within the company and traveled frequently on their behalf meeting people all over the world. My responsibility within the company included management of teams who, when I think of them now, were all more Resourceful Orange than I was. That made our meetings quite interesting at times, but usually with successful results. They were always in the spirit of fun and good humour, but with our goals, targets, and expectations strongly in sight.

In the latter part of my career, I decided that I needed a change. I had spent all of my time working for others in the same industry and decided that a complete change would be an exciting and healthy challenge. For some unknown reason I decided that I wanted my own business in a specialist retail field. After some searching I found one – it was in the, at that time new, field of on premises wine making. I took over a relatively new store with a small existing clientele and after a very short period became so busy that I had to hire more staff to assist with the day to day activities. At that time, the law had not been clarified and we worked on the assumption that we could offer samples to help customers make their decisions. Here I was in my element hosting wine tasting sessions for groups of a dozen or so almost every night. This lasted for a couple of years until I finally decided that the Resourceful Orange personality might have been the right person to be the party host and chief salesman but some other shade had to be in the back room taking care of the books and staff. The legal requirements also became clear and we were no longer able to hold sampling parties. The skills of a Resourceful Orange were no longer required so I came to my senses and returned to the industry that I knew and loved.

Impact of Extraversion on my Temperament:

Has being an extraverted Resourceful Orange in my chosen career been an advantage – you bet! An element in all of my positions has been meeting new people and developing effective relationships with them. This has suited me very well as I really enjoy interacting with people and I have a knack for building relationships. Quite frequently, my clients and work associates have become my friends. I know that I was always seen by others including my family as being outgoing and one who could be, if I choose to be, the life of the party. I know this would be dependent on any number of things but I always enjoyed a party.

Resourceful Oranges at Work

The Resourceful Orange Leader

Resourceful Oranges can be tough-minded leaders who are gifted at working with tools to achieve their goals. The tools they work with may be people, language, equipment, technology, or machinery. Being action-oriented, they will act quickly using the best means available to achieve practical results. They are in their element when quick, decisive leadership is required such as rescuing a company from bankruptcy or turning a dysfunctional department around. When multi-tasking they are in their element and love to have several balls in the air at the same time.

They are skilful negotiators and trouble shooters. Because of their ability to be in the "here and now", they are excellent at putting out fires, cleaning up messy situations, and leading in crises. In these situations, they demonstrate self-confidence and a sense of sureness about their actions that encourages others to follow them. Gifted negotiators, Resourceful Oranges can usually find the advantage and know what tactics to use to close the deal. To them negotiation is a highly exciting game and they really know how to play it well.

As leaders, they are pragmatic and realistic. Unlike other leaders, they deal with concrete problems and are not constrained by the past, rules, organizational structure, relationships, or the future. They give themselves the freedom to do what they need to do to solve problems and resolve issues. Having keen powers of observation, they can quickly assess what is really happening in an organization. When there are problems, they don't believe in over analyzing the situation – they act quickly to get things back on track. When it comes to organizational politics, Resourceful Oranges are masters at playing the political game. Generally not bucking the system, they work within it to accomplish results.

Resourceful Orange's coaching style is to lead by example. They are exceptionally dedicated, hard working leaders and expect their followers to be the same. When coaching their followers, they are more likely to demonstrate what to do rather than tell how to do it. They truly believe in leading and coaching by example. They will give their followers opportunities to practice and then give very specific feedback by focusing on what went well and what the follower needs to work on. The feedback will usually be given in a clear, no-nonsense manner. Resourceful Orange coaches set clear expectations for their followers, and then act as cheerleaders.

When leading organizations through change, Resourceful Oranges can be very effective. Because they are highly adaptable, they welcome and embrace change.[22] Most don't believe in worrying unnecessarily about things that they cannot control. To them it is more important to focus on the things that they can control and everything else will unfold as it needs to. Change is actually energizing to Resourceful Oranges, and most are more than willing to take risks as they make changes and will encourage others to do so as well. They don't worry too much about making mistakes because they usually have the ability to correct them quickly. However, their focus tends to be the present and they are less interested in strategic, long term change.

Resourceful Oranges are often quite competitive, and believe in motivating people through competition.[23]   Winning is important to them and they will happily compete with other leaders in their organization, their field, or even with mythical heroes. Similarly, they will motivate their followers by challenging them to perform better than their peers or even to beat their own records.

"Catalyst for action" is often how Resourceful Oranges are seen on the leadership team. They can be very persuasive and excel at verbal problem solving in the moment. Excellent negotiators, they are often able to work out an agreement that all team members can agree on. Resourceful Oranges tend to have a great sense of humour. Their humour along with their sense of camaraderie with their peers allows them to move the team forward especially during difficult and stressful times.

As leaders, Resourceful Oranges may pay a heavy price for their "in the moment" action orientation. Sometimes they act too quickly before truly understanding the big picture and the long term consequences of their actions. As a result some of their short term solutions may lead to problems that are more complex later on. While they enjoy setting a plan in motion, sometimes they may not follow through and consequently important tasks may not be completed.

At times, their leadership style can be seen as abrasive and domineering by the other Temperaments. Resourceful Oranges tend to dislike opposition because they see it as slowing down the process and not allowing them to get on with what needs to be done. Often they get frustrated with some of the other Temperaments because they move too slowly, focus overly on people concerns or question the Resourceful Orange leader's short term focus.

While Resourceful Oranges are highly effective trouble-shooters, they are less effective at maintaining the status quo in an organization. Because of their dislike for routine day to day work they can seem unpredictable, unprepared, and even irresponsible. Setting long term goals or maintaining rules, procedures, and organizational routines are not enjoyable. As a matter of fact, this type of leadership can be so boring to them that some actually go looking for trouble so that they can have some excitement in their life.

Tips for Working for a Resourceful Orange Leader

- Present your ideas in clear language and get to the point quickly
- Use humour
- Demonstrate that you are adaptable
- Do not expect to be micromanaged
- Use your initiative – once the task is assigned run with it and only ask questions if really necessary
- Demonstrate that you can make use of your skills in crisis situation
- Be willing to have fun at work
- Don't take offence, as Resourceful Orange leaders can be abrasive
- Be open to change
- Be prepared to work hard and play hard
- Create a competitive environment – they like to play the game
- Be proactive
- When presenting an idea demonstrate the practical benefits

The Resourceful Orange Employee

Resourceful Oranges are hard workers and take pride in getting things right -preferably the first time. These two things go a long way towards making them ideal employees.

However, they need to have freedom to achieve their work goals and do not like to be micromanaged.[24] If assigned a task they know how to do, they prefer if you tell them what needs to be done and by when, and they are allowed to figure out how it gets done. Given their work ethic, the task will be completed effectively and within the necessary time frame. If they need to learn new tasks, they learn best if you show them, and then let them do it, as they are hands-on tactile learners. Once shown how to do something, they flourish when left alone to do it. They will come back to the leader if they need additional help. However, they can become very frustrated and less productive if their leader micromanages their every action.

Time and enough space are very important to Resourceful Oranges; they value these in both their work and personal lives. They like to keep busy and don't like to have too much free time on their hands. If they do find themselves with free time, they will look for ways to fill it by taking on additional tasks or helping others. However, if they become bored and cannot find something productive to do they can get themselves into trouble. They don't have a need for control but don't like to feel as though they are being controlled. They tend to be very quick when it comes to reading people and situations and prefer to have the freedom and space to do things their own way.

Resourceful Oranges like to live life to its fullest and have a balance between work and fun. They pride themselves in doing a good job but also have a great need to have fun and seek out adventure. This will often lead them to look for ways to make their workplace more fun. Whether it is turning the task at hand into a competition of some kind, being part of the social committee, or decorating the office during a holiday season they just want to make life as enjoyable as possible for themselves and those around them.

Strong, bold, and assertive are words that others often use to describe a Resourceful Orange. They tend to take charge especially in crisis situations. Their unique ability to observe, assess, and analyze a situation enables them to make a decision and quickly act on it. Depending on their work environment, this can be either a great help or a hindrance. In a fast paced or crisis environment (such as an emergency room or a production support team) this can be extremely useful – especially if they are in a position where they can lead the team through the situation. However, if they hold a lower position in a rule-bound, hierarchical structure, both the Resourceful Orange and the rest of the organization can become frustrated. Resourceful Oranges do understand the need for structure and planning and they are willing to work within them when the rules make sense to them. However, they don't tend to see the need for all the rules and regulations they encounter in their day to day lives. They will often question, bend, or break these rules when they don't make sense.

Resourceful Oranges tend to make decisions quickly and don't like to waste time with the lengthy decision making process that often exists in many organizations. They don't see the need for drawn out discussions, decisions by committee, or multiple layers of approvals. They usually have the ability to quickly sum up the situation and make a decision. They often don't understand why others can't do the same thing. This can be advantageous if they are working in an environment where decisions need to be made and implemented quickly. However, Resourceful Oranges can become frustrated when the decision making process takes too long – especially when too many people have to be involved.

Being a team member in the workplace is not always a Resourceful Orange's favourite place to be (even though they can function well as part of a team). Resourceful Oranges are independent and sometimes avoid close personal ties with others as they like to have the freedom to do things their own way and this is not always possible as a team member. In addition, at times, they can find Organized Golds to be too structured and rule bound, Authentic Blues to be overly sensitive, and Inquiring Greens to be thoughtless and superficial.

Resourceful Oranges tend to excel when they can use their creative and persuasive skills. One of their many strengths is promoting ideas and products. They can often read people and situations and then respond quickly to them. Their ability to determine what the other person needs out of a situation allows them to work creatively to persuade the other person that an idea or product will meet their needs. These skills also work well for them in negotiations. A Resourceful Orange will usually negotiate from a win/win perspective ensuring that both their and the other person's needs are met.

Resourceful Oranges are generally happy when they work in environments that are fast paced and allow them the freedom to do a good job in the manner they best see fit.

Tips for Managing a Resourceful Orange Employee

- Use plain, clear language and get to the point quickly
- Use humour
- Be concise: only give the information that is useful and necessary to get the job done
- Make sure the task involves action

- Make sure the position involves variety
- Tell what you want accomplished, not how to do it
- Do not micromanage
- Allow them the freedom to make the job their own
- Make use of their skills in crisis situations
- Make them feel part of the team
- Create a competitive environment – they like to play the game
- They thrive in an environment where they can have fun

Resourceful Orange Superstars

Ronald Reagan

Ronald Reagan is an example of a Resourceful Orange who was successful not only as an actor but also as a politician. He was the 40th President of the United States from 1981 to 1989 and the 33rd Governor of California from 1967–1975.

Like many extraverted Resourceful Oranges, Reagan was known as a skilful performer and communicator. He was able to perfect these abilities in his earlier careers as a radio announcer, actor, and TV personality. As president, he was able to engage the American public through his speeches, his ability to tell stories and his personal charisma.

As president, Ronald Reagan pursued and implemented policies that reflected his belief in individual freedom. On the domestic front, he sought to stimulate the economy with large-scale tax cuts, giving people the freedom to spend their money as they saw fit, not as the government did. On the international front, he worked hard to end the cold war helping to free individuals from the constraints of communism.

He was a masterful negotiator and promoter and his effective use of these skills certainly contributed to the end of the cold war. He believed that if he could persuade the Soviets to allow for more democracy and free speech, this would lead to reform and the end of Communism. Reagan met the Russian leader, Mikhail Gorbachev on several occasions and made the first major move forward in the Cold War when they jointly agreed to get rid of some of their nuclear weapons. The Berlin Wall was torn down beginning in 1989 and two years later the Soviet Union collapsed.

Typical of many Resourceful Oranges, Reagan was an optimistic, good natured and fun loving person. He had a great sense of humour and was known for his numerous jokes and one-liners.[25]

Richard Branson

Richard Branson, the flamboyant British entrepreneur, is another example of a Resourceful Orange.

A true entrepreneur, he flourishes at starting new businesses. From an early age his entrepreneurial genius was apparent; he started his first business at 16, when he published a magazine called *Student*. Even today he is always on the look out for new opportunities and thrives on a challenge such as entering markets dominated by a few key players.

With his flamboyant and competitive style Richard Branson has created one of the most recognizable brands in the world. He has managed to "Virginize" a very wide range of products and services ranging from Virgin airlines, Virgin credit cards, Virgin books, to Virgin trains.

Like some Resourceful Oranges he enjoys performing on both television and in film. He has been a guest on several television shows such as "Friends", "Baywatch", and "Birds of a Feather", where he has played himself. He was also the star of a reality TV show called "The Rebel Billionaire: Branson's Quest for the Best".   In this show contestants were tested for their entrepreneurship and sense of adventure.

Richard Branson is a natural risk taker and adventurer. Always ready to try something new, he especially enjoys physical activity. He thrives on excitement, risk taking, and action. Since 1985 he has been meeting his need for adventure by attempting to break world records in boating and hot air ballooning. He has achieved several distance and speed records. However, he has yet to achieve his goal of being the first person to circumnavigate the world in a hot air balloon.[26]

Céline Dion

Céline Dion is a Canadian singer, songwriter, actress, and entrepreneur who has risen to international stardom as a contemporary pop vocalist.

Like many Resourceful Oranges, Céline Dion is a skilful performer who has worked tirelessly to perfect her ability as a singer. Renowned for her technical skills and powerful vocals, she dazzles her audiences with her voice and overall presentation.

She has used her creativity and ingenuity to make an impact on others. She demonstrated this desire to stand out from the crowd when planning her wedding to her manager René Angélil. Married at Caesar's Palace Casino and Hotel in Las Vegas, they decorated the hotel's chapel to look like an Arabian mosque. There was also an Arabian theme at the reception with tents, camels, imported birds, jugglers, and dancers. Céline Dion has also demonstrated her love of spectacle in her work life. For example, in 2002 she signed a three-year contract to appear five nights a week in an entertainment extravaganza in Las Vegas. The show introduced a new form of entertainment consisting of a mix of song, dance, theatrical innovation, and state-of-the-art technology.

Throughout her life, she has demonstrated flexibility and adaptability. In her late teens she recognized the need to makeover her image to achieve her goals of worldwide stardom. She subsequently underwent dental surgery to improve her appearance and received training to improve her English. This enabled her to successfully break into the English market and become an international superstar. In 2000, she announced a temporary retirement from entertainment in order to start a family and spend time with her husband, who was dealing with cancer. After her return to the spotlight, her work had matured again with new themes such as maternal bonds and brotherly love.
Céline Dion is an entrepreneur in her own right who is willing to take risks. She established her franchise restaurant "Nickels" in 1990. Additionally, she has a range of eyewear and a line of perfume manufactured by Coty.[27]

4

Organized Gold

Needs and Values

The key to the Organized Gold's sense of self worth is belonging,[28] whether it is to their family, work, or social group. Many of their actions are directed toward enhancing this sense of belonging. Family is so important that they often believe that looking after them is the most important thing that they do. Both at work and in the community they like to have membership in various groups as it helps them feel secure and needed. At work they gravitate towards membership in groups such as sports teams, social clubs, or the United Way. In the community they are usually active members of the groups that they value. Because a sense of belonging is so important to this Temperament they can suffer if they feel abandoned or isolated.

More than any of the other Temperament Organized Golds value security.[29] They feel that being as prepared as possible for potential problems is the best way they can show their love for those they care about. They will actively work to ensure that things go as planned and make contingency plans in case of problems. Their motto in life "be prepared", is an excellent descriptor of their natural planning abilities.

Organized Golds appreciate good leadership. They believe that a strong leader at the helm of any organization enables that organization to grow and prosper. They also believe in the importance of hierarchical structures. Their view is once the leader has set the direction there should be a chain of command where everyone has clearly defined roles and responsibilities. Organized Golds often admire institutions such as the monarchy, religious institutions, or the military because of the traditions these organizations embrace and their ability to continue having them flourish through generations. Indeed, they often aspire to leadership positions themselves and can make able leaders in politics, education, and business.

They embrace duty and responsibility, believing that if everyone contributes their fair share then the world will be a more stable and equitable place. Towards that end, Organized Golds take responsibility for family, work, and community very seriously. They do what they say they are going to do and always do their best to meet their commitments.

Organized Golds understand the need for positive recognition. They will work tirelessly for others in the hope that they will be recognized and appreciated for what they do. Indeed, they often end up performing tasks that others prefer not to do such as taking out the garbage, paying the bills, or getting the car serviced. However, they can end up feeling resentful if others take them for granted and don't give them the recognition that they feel they deserve.

Strengths

Planning and organizing skills are great strengths of the Organized Golds. At home or at work they are able to look at what they need to accomplish, set priorities, and develop an action plan. The action plan will define the steps everyone needs to take to accomplish the task. They will then work conscientiously to achieve their plan. Often time management whizzes they will use "to do" lists, prioritizing techniques, goal setting, diaries, BlackBerries® and other tools to accomplish their goals. They are very conscious of time and pride themselves on always being punctual. Because they take pride in being punctual, they can get frustrated with others who are late.

Common sense thinking is another strength that Organized Golds bring to the table. They rarely make irrational decisions. Rather they use sound judgment and logical thinking based on the facts of the situation. Others generally perceive them as level headed and not prone to flights of fancy. They tend to look to the past to see what has worked in similar situations for inspiration in how to deal with current problems.

They are dependable, reliable, hard working and keep their word by getting their children to school on time, completing their job conscientiously, paying their bills on time, and generally obeying the rules of society. Another saying that many Organized Golds live by is "work now, play later." They get a sense of accomplishment from achieving their tasks and only after they have finished would they think about relaxing and enjoying themselves.

Often believing in excellence, they have high standards for themselves and others, especially when it comes to order and quality. You just need to look at an Organized Gold's home or workspace to determine that one lives there. You will usually see a neat, orderly environment with everything in its proper place. Their striving for excellence often demonstrates itself in attention to detail. They are good at reviewing highly detailed work, picking up mistakes and correcting them, believing that improvement is always possible. Once an Organized Gold has observed a mistake they are competent at giving feedback to improve the work.

Because they have a strong need for belonging and they believe in helping others, Organized Golds are cooperative and willing team members. They enjoy the camaraderie of working with others, contributing tirelessly to any group to which they belong. They bring to the table their planning and organizing skills making sure the group accomplishes tasks in an orderly fashion and does not forget to do anything important. Additionally, they tend to go the extra mile, working hard to ensure the team outcome is successful.

Organized Golds provide cultural stability by maintaining the traditions of their family and community. At home, they will spend a lot of time and energy on traditions like Christmas, Hanukah, Thanksgiving, and Diwali. For example, for Thanksgiving some Organized Golds will enjoy collecting decorations, tablecloths and other items that make the celebration special. They will make sure that birthdays and anniversaries are celebrated. In the community they support and work for organizations such as Scouting, their place of worship, and parent teacher associations.

Potential Challenges

Organized Golds, especially extreme ones see it as their duty in life to uphold quality in everything. Unfortunately, as a means of doing this they often use criticism or become authoritarian. In their eyes, they are just doing their duty. However, to the other Temperaments this criticism can seem harsh and unwarranted.[30] Others can view Organized Golds as uncompromising and dictatorial. Many Organized Golds believe that they are being helpful providing feedback on quality, as they themselves would appreciate. Therefore, they are more likely to criticise than to give praise, tending to believe there is always room for improvement and you only give praise when there is no room to improve. Because of this "I know best" approach to life many of the other Temperaments resist what the Organized Golds have to say or even just ignore them. This is very difficult for Organized Golds because they need recognition for their contributions and when they don't get it they can become resentful and bitter.

Organized Gold followers – especially extreme ones – can be too willing to follow. They are respectful of authority, at times are not willing to voice dissent even if they do not agree. Sometimes they are so respectful of their leaders they are willing to do anything they are told to do, forgetting to challenge when the task does not make sense or is unsafe.

Because of their strong sense of responsibility Organized Golds often live in, what they describe as, a constant state of anxiety. Instead of looking on the bright side of life they can be prone to taking a very pessimistic view of things. Some constantly worry about what could go wrong next and then make sure they are prepared for it. For example, if planning a family outing to a water park the Organized Golds will make sure everyone has sunscreen and umbrellas, and that the children all wear hats and sun protective swimwear. A day of fun and enjoyment can happen as long as other duties have been addressed, resolved and there is a plan to complete it in the future. They are also likely to ensure sure there is an education component to the day. The other Temperaments can find the Organized Gold's negative outlook saps the fun and enjoyment out of life. They can be so overprotective, and at times rigid, that the other Temperaments feel smothered by them.

Many Organized Golds tend to take the weight of the world on their shoulders. Whether at work or at home they are the ones that everyone depends on to get things done or hold everything together. This is because the Organized Golds will go that extra mile, take on extra tasks and do whatever it takes to make sure the job is done and done right. The problem is they run the risk of being overworked and sometimes even overwhelmed to the point of exhaustion.

Overwork and exhaustion are common problems for an Organized Gold. It is not unusual to hear them ask "Well if I don't do it, who will?" They are often unwilling to not do a task if they feel that it would make them appear in a negative light. However, because of their sense of responsibility they will do whatever it takes to make sure no one knows how they are feeling. Additionally, they are unlikely to ask for help because they like to appear in control at all times. In the long run this can lead to exhaustion, burnout, and even physical illness. Often there are no physical signs of exhaustion or burnout. It is often difficult for the other Temperaments to recognize the signs because as Organized Golds gets more overwhelmed they tend to look better and better, often paying more attention to the way they look and the way they present themselves to the world. It is very important to them that no one knows how close to the edge they are so they put on a very brave front to the rest of the world. Sometimes it is not until it is too late that others realize how desperate things are for the Organized Gold.

Change tends not to be an Organized Gold's friend. They like life to be orderly and stable. For them routine is good because everyone knows what they are supposed to do and how they should be doing it. Today's world can cause much anxiety for Organized Golds because everything is changing at a fairly rapid pace. We tend to live in a society that is constantly moving forward, one that puts more value in looking towards the future and the next innovation than the past and traditions. This can be uncomfortable for Organized Golds and as a result, others often perceive them as very negative towards life. They need to learn strategies to embrace changes by understanding the benefits of new methods. Other Temperaments may distance themselves because they fear rejection, criticism, or abuse.

In Their Own Words

In this section, an introverted and extraverted Organized Gold describe their Temperament in their own words:

An Introverted Organized Gold

My needs and values:

- *Family, belonging, loyalty – favourite animal – musk ox – very protective of the family*
- *Member of United Way committee and on the Ontario Association for the Application of Personality Type Board of directors*
- *Don't feel bad if you don't love me or want a close relationship but very hurt if you dislike me or don't care at all*
- *A relationship with an Inquiring Green leaves me feeling marginalized and partially abandoned*
- *One weekend my eldest daughter, her boyfriend and my other daughter decided to take a weekend trip to Perth, Ontario to visit my family. I drove my youngest daughter to meet the other two at Queen's Quay downtown Toronto, their takeoff point. I asked if they had a map, turned out they only had MapQuest and that was actually partially inaccurate. So, I handed over a map and as it was 4:00pm on a Friday and I instructed them to listen to 680 News Radio till they got out of Toronto for the traffic reports every 10 minutes. I phoned them twice on route to see if all was well and Saturday night after I figured they would have left my sister's BBQ I phoned my sister to see how things went. To my shock, my daughter answered and said, "Are you checking up on me?" to which I replied "Ahhh – sorry wrong number!" She said "Busted Dad – they have digital display!" I didn't dare check to see if they arrived home safely but I did ask my sister to ask mom if the kids had phoned.*
- *Like a conservative approach to business – hierarchy with good leadership – fair and consistent with lots of rules and regulations to fall back on or at least guidelines*
- *Also like structure, authority (benevolent), sense of right and wrong*

- *Much prefer a behind the scenes role rather than leader*
- *Duty and responsibility is always there and sometimes out of guilt*
- *Persevere with commitments – won't stop till complete*
- *At home roles have almost reversed – I do the garbage, pay most of the bills, servicing of cars, lawns and gardens, snow shovelling, vacuuming, dishes, most of the cooking, laundry, and maintenance and yes I do feel taken for granted at times.*
- *Like lists*

My strengths:

- *Like to plan and organize*
- *I am a list maker*
- *I love to be punctual and would rather be early*
- *A purist – don't like knock-off's, imitations, watered-down versions or 2nd runner-up alternatives – originals please*
- *Historically based, I also have the largest filing system of anyone at work*
- *Detailed – boss once said "Paul you are a pain in the ass to work with but you have saved my butt so many times!"*
- *Tend to appear level headed, laid back, and a good listener – although stress can turn all that around*
- *Work now, play later – last vacation was 4 years ago – this summer spent 3 weeks working on refinishing my deck*
- *High standards – find it easy to critique or edit*
- *I have been a coach/mentor for programs at work*
- *I will work hard to make someone else look good and shun the limelight*
- *I hate seeing traditions fall and disagree with our modern liberalism*
- *I celebrate traditional holidays with family as much as I can – I try not to miss birthdays and anniversaries and was upset when my family decided to do away with Christmas gifts*
- *Dependable and stabilizing – sober second thought, anchor*

- *Warm-hearted, sympathetic, and giving*
- *I have a disabled daughter called Tara – my ex has been quoted as saying "Tara is with the wrong parent"*
- *Shy – with strangers – may appear stiff, cold or aloof – actually often a sign of sincerity*
- *Can talk a lot and topic hop with close friends/relatives*

My potential challenges:

- *It does not bother me if I am not recognized, but don't stomp on my values and principles*
- *I can become a willing follower but from an "avoid conflict at all costs" approach*
- *Very anxious – major worrier – cup is half empty*
- *I believe I am burnt out at work from years of going the extra mile and not getting the recognition – I try to 'smell the roses' a little more – despite the flack*
- *Bed late every night – too many things, duties, to take care of – always tired – getting 4 – 5 hours sleep a night over the last 4 or 5 years*
- *I hate change for the sake of change – give me time, support, information, benefits and I can deal with most change – however that is not usually how the business world works*
- *I can become a doormat*
- *Vagueness or lack of detail, constant noise, loud noise, busy, noisy background disrupt my thinking – go into shell, become quiet, senses shut down, solitude – sometimes a fleeting panic moment*
- *Overly cautious*
- *Under stress – lots of aches and pains*

Impact of Introversion on my Temperament:

- *I have social skills and like people but shy away from some types of socializing. Chitchat at social gatherings is a pain. I avoid* crowds and make a mandatory appearance at the staff Christmas party and leave

- *Tend to be a wall-flower at large gatherings and find a safe place to perch until another percher is spotted*
- *Enjoy one-on-one as large groups are energy draining*
- *At the end of a day of teaching I am exhausted*
- *I am not a major joiner and have to be very interested, asked, and yes even goaded into a membership, position, etc.*
- *Often find that my suggestions are not taken seriously and others can say the same thing to great acclaim*
- *Try to slow extraverts down*
- *Over prepare – to avoid brain lock*
- *Cautious and passive – often this is misinterpreted or misread as aloof, mysterious or snobby – boss could never figure me out*
- *Don't talk a lot unless asked, therefore I don't get much feedback that acknowledges that I am knowledgeable in certain areas*
- *A few close friends*
- *Shut down external stimuli when overwhelmed – also need time to internally compare what's going on with past experiences*
- *Reflective – slower pace – longer to react – big picture first – long term memory*
- *Don't blow own horn*
- *In a meeting hard to absorb new info and offer an opinion – "I will go away and formulate an opinion rather than conjure one up right now"*

An Extraverted Organized Gold

My needs and values:

As an Organized Gold, I first and foremost need to feel that I belong. My family is one of the most important aspects of my life and plays a key role in providing the sense of belonging that I require. I will often take on tasks that others avoid and regularly make an effort to do something special for a member of the family such as give someone a *present for no reason at all or plan a surprise party. I get pleasure from making others feel special. In return, I need recognition for my efforts. Often the small gestures that I perform to show I care go unnoticed and this can make me feel unappreciated and resentful.*

My need for belonging extends beyond the family. At work and in my community I look for organizations to join that will also make me feel needed. I gravitate towards organizations that work to help others. I feel a responsibility to be a valuable member of my community and enhance my self-worth through the recognition I receive from my volunteer work.

I believe that security, financial and physical, is tremendously important and I work to be prepared for any foreseeable situation. I feel most comfortable when I have a contingency plan. I always ensure that I have money put away in case of an emergency. I would never take a trip or make a large purchase without already having saved the money. I often worry about my finances and feel very uncomfortable and overwhelmed when a situation arises that was not planned.

My strengths:

I have an overwhelming sense of responsibility to everyone I am connected to and with everything that I do. I always put others before myself and find it difficult to say no. Regardless of the task I complete everything to the best of my ability. I believe that commitments are non-negotiable. No matter the cost to myself, whether personal or financial, I will meet the commitments I make. I feel like a failure if I am unable to deliver on a commitment. Because I so strongly value responsibility I expect others to also value and meet the commitments they have made. I expect everyone in the community to contribute and I become frustrated when I feel that others are neglecting their duties.

I have an unmatched ability for organization, planning, and multi-tasking. I love to make lists of all the tasks I need to complete and check off each item as I progress. I often complete tasks in advance of due dates. I excel at work because of my ability to prioritize and handle stress. I do not get overwhelmed when I have a number of projects to complete. My co-workers will often marvel at the speed and proficiency with which I complete tasks.

My strong sense of responsibility makes me a person that can be counted on. I am very hard working and reliable. I have an inability to relax if I have a task that needs to be completed. For example, if I plan to clean the house on Saturday this will be the first thing I do. I need to complete my responsibilities before taking time for myself. I will always go the extra step to help someone out. For this reason I am often a valued member of any group I join. In addition, I am very conscientious of time. I would rather arrive an hour early for an event than 30 seconds late. I become nervous and anxious if I am going to be late. I am very respectful of other people's time and do not want them to have to wait on me.

I set a high standard for myself, which is evident in the quality of work that I produce. I am very detail oriented and as a result, my work is most often error free. I always feel that I could have done better and improved my work. I am very critical of my work and myself. If I don't meet the level of excellence I desire I feel like a failure. My need for excellence is also reflected in my personal appearance and the tidiness of my work station and home. I feel it is very important to be well put together. I dislike anything being out of order. I am unable to concentrate on a task if my work station is messy. I love to challenge myself to prove that I can achieve the objective I have set out for myself. I look for new things to learn or do, always wanting to improve myself.

My potential challenges:

As a very organized and driven person who expects everything to be just right I can be too demanding of others. I often don't realize that my expectations are unrealistic. I have difficulty understanding why others don't complete tasks with the same sense of responsibility that I do. I often criticize the person for the errors they made rather than appreciating their efforts. I often have difficulty seeing the good intentions of a person and instead focus on the negative.

I can be very pessimistic. I have difficulty seeing the good in a situation. If something goes wrong I will blame myself regardless of whether or not I could control the situation. I worry about almost everything. I am constantly concerned about how others perceive me, the quality of my work, and the details around every day tasks. I spend so much time ensuring that I meet my responsibilities that I miss out on some of the best things in life.

I have difficulty saying no to people because I feel a responsibility to help anyone in need. As a result I end up overwhelmed with the amount of things I have agreed to do. I hate to fail or admit that I can't get something done. Instead, I will work to the point of exhaustion to meet my commitments. I don't want my stress to become the stress of others so I try to hide how I am feeling. I also don't feel that I can ask others for help when I was the one who agreed to complete the tasks. My desire to make everyone happy can come at the cost of my personal happiness and health. I also have difficulty relaxing. There is always something that I could be doing – cleaning, working, etc. I always want to be on the go. I don't have time to sit and enjoy the view. This can have a negative impact on my family because I project this need always to be "doing" something on to them so they miss out on relaxing.

Impact of extraversion on my Temperament:

My Temperament compliments my extrovert tendencies. My need for belonging causes me to seek out groups. As an extrovert I am energized by working in groups and talking with other people. As an Organized Gold I fulfill my need for outward action by constantly offering assistance to other people.

Extraversion can impact my Temperament negatively. As a person who often speaks my mind without thinking and one who can be overly critical, I can cause harm to people when I don't mean to. I often don't think through what I am going to say.

Organized Golds at Work

The Organized Gold Leader

The Organized Gold leader's supreme strength is in ensuring that an organization runs smoothly and efficiently. They will work within the existing organizational structure to create clear goals and objectives for their team by carefully planning what to do. They ensure that each follower knows specifically what to accomplish, how to do it and by when. To achieve this they develop a clear set of procedures, rules, and guidelines. The Organized Gold provides a stable, predictable environment where followers know what to expect and where they stand.

As leaders they have high standards for both themselves and others, leading by example. No one works harder or longer than an Organized Gold. Because of their high standards, they are effective at monitoring and managing the work of others. They believe in continuous improvement, and are effective teachers, showing how things should be done so that others can learn. They are comfortable giving employees constructive, specific feedback so that the employee can perform optimally. Sometimes others perceive Organized Golds as being very hard on them just because they believe that nothing is perfect and there is always room for improvement. Giving feedback is a natural process for Organized Golds; they have a need to give it as much as they have a need to receive it.

As a realist the Organized Gold leader knows that at any time, anything can and does go wrong. They are naturally cautious and security minded. Therefore they try to anticipate what could go wrong and put security measures and contingency plans in place to protect their followers and bring stability to the workplace. The well known saying about *Murphy's Law;* "Anything that can go wrong, will", was likely coined by the Organized Gold Leader.

They are decisive, practical, and do not suffer from analysis paralysis. However because of their cautious nature they need sufficient practical information and facts to make a sound decision. Theory or irrelevant information can overwhelm them. When making decisions they weigh all of the alternatives and base the decision on the available information, their past experience and knowledge of the traditions and policies of the organization.

Because Organized Golds tend to focus on the specifics in the here and now they can lack vision as leaders. They are much more comfortable focusing on the past and the present than on the future. Often they focus on concrete details rather than the big picture. Unlike the Inquiring Greens or the Authentic Blues, they don't usually imagine new possibilities and realities in the future. The Organized Gold leader will need to work hard to look at the big picture and the future direction of the organization rather than getting bogged down in the details of the past or present.

As leaders others don't perceive them as "early adopters" because they can sometimes seem rigid and resistant to change. What is true is that they don't jump on the bandwagon and accept change until they have thoroughly examined the circumstances to determine whether it is beneficial. Rather they are cautious because they don't want to "throw out the baby with the bath water." They want to hold onto what has worked well in the past and only implement those changes that they believe will improve the situation. Before they support change they want to work out the logistics in terms of what, when, and how to implement the change.

On the leadership team they provide the voice of practicality and common sense. They also ensure that all important details are considered. In these constantly changing times, they provide a necessary stability – challenging "change for the sake of change" without demonstrated reason. They also ensure that the team does not forget the important traditions of the organization. Finally, if the organization does not have traditions they will create them – the company picnic, golf tournament, holiday party, etc.

Tips for Working for an Organized Gold Leader

- Keep your work space tidy
- Work in a systematic way
- Present your ideas in a detailed manner
- Be punctual
- Do what you say your are going to do – keep your word
- Be prepared and open to criticism
- Stick to the standards and procedures
- Respect traditions and history
- Be prepared and efficient
- Demonstrate loyalty

- Be a team player and help others

- Complete tasks and see things through to completion

The Organized Gold Worker

Doing a job well and getting praise are two of the most important things in life for many Organized Golds. They want to feel as though they are an important part of their organization and that they are contributing to the smooth and efficient running of it. They strive to be successful and productive members of any team of which they are a part.

If you need a well organized person who is an effective administrator an Organized Gold is the person you are looking for. They are very good at taking on tasks which have a defined process, and/or meeting required milestones within a specific time frame; if there is not process, they are happy to create one. They are often attracted to positions in various types of administration, especially in the fields of medicine, public education, and social services. Because of their sense of duty and responsibility they often make great teachers, nurses, technicians, orderlies, and clerical staff. Organized Golds often enjoy positions such as museum curator, archivist, or librarian because of their attention to detail.

They have a strong sense of community and tradition and they bring it to any role they take on. As a teacher they tend to put a lot of emphasis on the basics of reading, writing, and arithmetic. They believe in teaching by rote with plenty of practice. For example, when teaching the alphabet they would use the ABCs song.

No matter what their job, it is important for an Organized Gold to feel they are performing useful tasks. They are also much more comfortable working in organizations that have a set structure and hierarchy, one with clear boundaries, set expectations, and time lines. They respond well to and respect authority. If they know the person asking them to do something is in a position of authority they will comply. When being assigned a task they prefer to know what the task is, how do it, when it is due, and if applicable, what the budget is. If they know these things they will go above and beyond to make sure they complete the task effectively using the specified procedure, on time, and within budget.

Jobs that require the ability to audit and work within a set of defined rules are often a good fit for an Organized Gold. They are frequently attracted to jobs such as the military or the police force because of the sense of duty and responsibility that goes along with serving their country or upholding the laws of the land.

When it comes to motivation, praise, rewards, recognition, and money often work well for Organized Golds. They tend to feel that earned money is more important than money that they have been given or won. This is because they see earned money as recognition of a job well done. They see this money as concrete proof that they are doing a good job and as a way of building a secure future for themselves and their families.

Overall, Organized Golds make a great addition to any organization and without them many organizations would just fall apart at the seams. The Organized Golds of the world keep everything running in an efficient and effective manner.

Tips for Managing an Organized Gold Employee

- Communicate clearly, logically, and sequentially
- Fill them in on the details of a task
- Provide an organized environment
- Give opportunities for practical application
- Hold them accountable for their actions
- Recognize accomplishments with tangible rewards e.g. lunch
- Where possible provide them with a predictable work environment
- Give them opportunities for purposeful and meaningful service
- Have set policies and procedures and seek feedback on revising and improving them
- Keep to your commitments as a leader
- Give them a sense of belonging

Organized Gold Superstars

Queen Elizabeth II

Elizabeth Alexandra Mary was born on the 21st of April, 1926. She became the Queen of the United Kingdom, Canada, Australia, New Zealand, South Africa, Pakistan, and Ceylon upon the death of her father, King George VI, on the 6th of February 1952. Her reign of 58 years is one of the longest in British history.[31]

Even as a child, she displayed the preferences of an Organized Gold. Marion Crawford, Princess Elizabeth's governess describes Elizabeth's orderliness and her attitude of responsibility in her book The Little Princesses. Winston Churchill also indicated that even as a very young child she had an air of authority. Finally, her cousin Margaret Rhodes described her as a sensible and well-behaved child.

From an early age community organizations were an important part of Princess Elizabeth's life. The 1st Buckingham Palace Girl Guides Company was formed specifically so she could socialize with girls her own age. She later enrolled as a Sea Ranger.
In 1945 her sense of duty caused her to join the Women's Auxiliary Territorial Service as No. 230873 Second Subaltern Elizabeth Windsor. There she trained as a driver and mechanic. She drove a military truck and rose to the rank of Junior Commander. Princess Elizabeth was the last surviving head of state to serve in uniform during World War II.

Since becoming the queen in 1952, Queen Elizabeth has been careful not to express her personal political opinions in a public forum. As would be expected from an Organized Gold she has maintained this discipline throughout her reign. She also has a deep sense of religious and civic duty, and takes her coronation oath seriously. As with most other Organized Golds, Queen Elizabeth is known for her conservative fashion sense. She tends to favour mostly off solid-colour overcoats and decorative hats, which allow her to be seen easily in a crowd.
Her main leisure interests tend to be fairly traditional, including horse racing, photography, and dogs, especially her Pembroke Welsh Corgis.

It would seem that Queen Elizabeth's sense of duty and tradition will keep her on the throne. In 2006 she made it clear that she had no intention of abdicating and Buckingham Palace announced that she would continue with her duties, both public and private, well into the future. This seems to be just fine with the majority of people in Britain, as polls in 2006 showed strong support for Elizabeth. Most wanted her to remain on the throne until her death and many felt that she had become an institution unto herself.

Wayne Gretzky

Wayne Douglas Gretzky was born on January 26, 1961 in Brantford, Ontario, Canada. Like many other Organized Golds, Gretzky set goals for himself at a young age and worked on perfecting his hockey skills at a backyard rink. This allowed him to regularly play minor hockey at a level far above his peers and go on to have one of the most successful hockey careers ever. He has been nicknamed "The Great One," and was called the greatest player of all time in *Total Hockey: The Official Encyclopedia of the NHL.* Gretzky is generally regarded as the best player in the history of the NHL.[32]

While with the Edmonton Oilers he established many scoring records and led the team to four Stanley Cup Championships. These are all important forms of recognition for an Organized Gold. When traded to the Los Angeles Kings his strong leadership skills had an immediate impact on their performance. He led them to the 1993 Stanley Cup finals, and it is said that because of him hockey became popular in the southern United States again, another important form of recognition for an Organized Gold.

The importance of his strong family ties was evident in comments he made to Scott Morrison about his final game. He indicated that everything he enjoyed about the sport of hockey as a kid – driving to practice and games with his mom and dad, seeing family and friends in the stand watching him as he played – all crystallized in his last game in New York

During his career, Gretzky received many awards. As mentioned earlier, these were important forms of recognition to him as an Organized Gold. The awards did not end with his retirement from the NHL. In 1999 he was inducted into the Hockey Hall of Fame.

After retiring from the NHL in 2000 he became part owner of the Phoenix Coyotes, and, after the 2004–05 NHL lockout, became their head coach, a position that he held until September 24, 2009. It was evident that his resignation was another demonstration of his Organized Gold tendencies to put the needs of others ahead of his own. Commissioner Gary Bettman agreed that he did indeed put the welfare of the team ahead of his own when he made that difficult decision.

The Organized Gold's structured leadership approach was again evident in 2002 when Gretzky became Executive Director of the Canadian National Men's Hockey team for the 2002 Winter Olympics where the team won a gold medal.

He was asked to manage Canada's team at the 2005 Ice Hockey World Championships, but he put family before his career and declined because of his mother's poor health.

Julia Child

Julia Child was born on August 15, 1912 as Julia Carolyn McWilliams. She was an American chef, author and television personality. Julia is credited with introducing French cuisine and cooking techniques to the American mainstream through her many cookbooks and TV programs.[33]

After the bombing of Pearl Harbor, like many other Organized Golds, Julia's sense of responsibility led her to serve her country. When she found she was too tall to enlist in the Women's Army Corps (WACs) or in the U.S. Navy through the Women Accepted for Volunteer Emergency Service (WAVES) she joined the Office of Strategic Services (OSS). Later in her career while posted to China she received the Emblem of Meritorious Civilian Service as head of the Registry of the OSS Secretariat. This recognition for her service would have been very important to her as an Organized Gold.

On September 1, 1946 Julia married Paul Cushing Child in Lumberville, Pennsylvania. Despite her Organized Gold's love of family the couple was unfortunately unable to have children.

She perfected her cooking skills while living in Paris. She attended the famous Le Cordon Bleu cooking school and then studied privately with Max Bugnard and other master chefs. As an Organized Gold, having a sense of community was important to her so she joined the women's cooking club Cercle des Gourmettes where she met Simone Beck and her friend, Louisette Bertholle. Beck and Bertholle were writing a French cookbook for Americans and proposed that Julia work with them to make it appeal to Americans. For the next 10 years they researched and repeatedly tested recipes to make them perfect. Because of Julia's Organized Gold abilities they were able to translate the French into English, make the recipes detailed, interesting, and practical. The book, *Mastering the Art of French Cooking*, was finally published in 1961. It became a best seller and received critical acclaim. It is still in print today and is considered a seminal culinary work.

In 1981, her Organized Gold need to see traditions continued led her to found the educational American Institute of Wine and Food in Napa, California, with vintners Robert Mondavi and Richard Graff. The purpose of the institute was to advance the understanding, appreciation and quality of wine and food.

In 2001, upon moving to a retirement community, her Organized Gold sense of tradition led her to donate her kitchen, which was the set for three of her television series, to the National Museum of American History where it is now on display.

5

Authentic Blue

Needs and Values

One of the major driving forces for Authentic Blues is self-actualization. They are always trying to improve themselves by attending courses, reading, or talking with others. Finding meaning and significance in their personal and professional life is an ongoing quest.

Over time, they have developed a set of values that help them to achieve these needs. With a strong belief in human potential, Authentic Blues tend to gravitate to situations where they can help others grow and develop. For example, they are more likely to choose professions such as teaching or counselling where they can contribute to society in a meaningful way.

One of their values is to look for the positive in others. They are much more likely to put their faith in a person than to search for their faults. Some can see this as gullible, but by having this attitude toward their fellow human beings, they are much more able to build relationships based on mutual trust and respect.

Of all of the Temperaments, the Authentic Blues tend to be the most spiritual, however, that does not necessarily mean they are attracted to mainstream religions. Many are more attracted to alternative spiritual practices such as meditation. They will often refer to themselves as humanists in that they want to lead meaningful, ethical lives and contribute to the greater good of humanity.

They see themselves as unique and want others to acknowledge their individuality. Their unique identity may show itself in the clothes they wear, the lifestyle they choose, the way they furnish their home, or the way they interact with others.

Relationships are very important to Authentic Blues and these relationships must be empathic and meaningful. They only consider a person to be a friend once they truly get to know and accept each other – warts and all. For introverted Authentic Blues this can take quite a bit of time. They do not like to live in conflict, preferring to build bridges with and between others so that they can live a life that is full of harmony and unity.

The old saying "two heads are better than one" is very true of this Temperament. They enjoy working in a synergistic and creative way with others because they believe that the results will be much better.[34] Their imagination enables them to come up with innovative ways to understand and resolve problems.

Authentic Blues strive to be authentic and genuine in all that they do and expect others to be the same. They live by their values and strong code of ethics and it can cause them pain if they have to go against one of their ethics or principles. Authentic Blues can get very angry if they observe what they believe to be unethical behaviour in others. The extraverts are more likely to engage actively in some form of protest against this type of behaviour.

Strengths

Authentic Blues often excel in communicating with others. They are able to use language to express themselves in a persuasive way and they can be gifted in the use of stories, analogies, and metaphors. As an empathetic listener they can often see the deeper layers in what others are saying. This is because they are not only attuned to the words that a person is using, but also their body language, facial expression, and tone of voice. When interacting with Authentic Blues, others really feel heard and understood. Authentic Blues are quick to praise when it is genuinely deserved and others see them as supportive and caring.

When it comes to identifying and developing the potential of others Authentic Blues are at their best. Whether their role is the team leader or a team member they have a natural talent to help the team work cohesively to achieve their goals. They enjoy situations where they can help people identify their purpose in life, and work with and support them in achieving that purpose. An Authentic Blue can be a good coach, mentor, co-worker, and friend.

They are intuitive and use this ability in both individual and group situations. Authentic Blues are able to see what others are often not able regarding what is really happening with the individual or group. They may have a vague sense of what is happening or a crystal clear vision. They may not be able to explain to others why they know, but in most situations, they are correct about what is going on.

Authentic Blues naturally gravitate towards conceptual information and the big picture. They look towards the future and are therefore ideally suited to helping others fulfill their potential. They are able to look at information from various perspectives and integrate it into a unified theme. By using their intuition and big picture perspective they often see connection and patterns that are not always clear to others.

Most Authentic Blues tend to be imaginative and artistic which shows up in all aspects of their lives. At work, they have the ability to generate new ideas and possibilities at times coming up with a different way of looking at a situation and approaching it. At home, they are often interested in interior design which will lead them to create a unique and inviting environment.

Of all the Temperaments, they are the most altruistic.[35] They believe that happiness comes from giving to others and this is why they often end up in helping professions such as counselling or teaching. To help others, even if they have to make sacrifices to do so, helps Authentic Blues meet their basic need of self-actualization.

Authentic Blues usually make great additions to any teams. Whether it as the team leader or as a team member their ability to communicate effectively, see issues from all sides, and bring harmony to any situation makes them a great asset. When conflict arises they are often able to mediate the situation and gain resolution.

Potential Challenges

Authentic Blues may be overly sensitive to criticism and conflict. Because they prefer to live in a harmonious environment they can take negative feedback very personally. Unlike other Temperaments they don't separate themselves from their behaviour so they tend to take criticism to heart. They can also be overly self-critical if they perceive that they have failed in some way. They are finely attuned to conflict; however, they do not enjoy dealing with it. Because conflict makes them feel so uncomfortable they may try to avoid it or accommodate others rather than confront problems.

Because of their global perspective, Authentic Blues may have a tendency to use overstatement in the language that they use. For example instead of saying something went "well" they might say, "it went fantastically." They may also have difficulty describing things in a detailed manner. For example, if asked to describe a room they are more likely to describe the atmosphere or feeling of the room rather than the colour of the sofa or the number of pictures on the walls.

As a result of their ability to see connections and patterns they can sometimes make assumptions based on only limited facts. This can get them into trouble if they act on these incorrect assumptions rather than checking out their validity before acting.

Because Authentic Blues are dedicated to people issues and want harmony they may spend too much time working on the process of how people work together rather than focusing on the task at hand. This can lead to issues with time management and goal achievement.

Their relationship needs and desire to help others grow and develop can cause Authentic Blues to have a tendency to be "overly helpful." By that, we mean that they may continue to support a person even after the person is able to stand on their own two feet because of their need to maintain the relationship. Alternatively, it could mean that they find it difficult to say "No" and as a result may overload themselves with too much work and ultimately burn out.

In Their Own Words

In this section, an introverted and extraverted Authentic Blue describe their Temperament in their own words:

An Introverted Authentic Blue

My needs and values:

To me, being a "blue" I think my most important needs and values are those that manifest themselves from another place, e.g., "out of the blue". For this is where inspiration, pre-cognitions, intuition, empathy, and deep compassion emerge. In Hinduism, Krishna is represented as an Authentic Blue heavenly being who engages with His followers on many levels helping them find their voice, their song, their rhythm, their dance and their place.

Congruency in words and actions are really important to me. Having the heart and the mouth speak in a congruent way and truthful way is essential. I value keeping my word.

A few friends, deeply connected, satisfy me. I don't need lots of friends or acquaintances, but I do need depth of relationship, understanding, and communication.

Blue as the sky, Deep as the ocean, Wider than the sky, and beyond realms we can imagine Blue breathes Life into the parched soul, giving it rest and respite With its deep healing waters...

My strengths and potential challenges:

My strengths and challenges are similar. Because I may intuit answers, situational options, and I think quickly and act quickly, I may on occasion be impulsive, and I get hurt or angry when others don't understand the solution I have intuited without all the facts.

Impact of Introversion on my Temperament:

I find it easier to listen and give empathy than to try to get listened to. Extraverts appear to me to take up all the space, all the words, and all the energy. Yet still waters run deep. I learned a long time ago that when in fact an introvert gets the invitation to speak you had better say it fast and quick for just that fast some orange extrovert will jump in and take over the words, the space, etc. and you will be just sitting waiting for your next turn to speak, which of course may or may not happen.

I value ideas, and often enjoy ideas more than people, although I do love most people, but I find them tiring very quickly. Being blue is mysticism, in the heavenly realm, spiritual, loving, and thank goodness this is only part of my Temperaments.

Put me in the company of blues, golds, and greens, where we can think, listen, be creative, and put our energy on bigger ideas, concepts, and universalities. Give me time to pause, to ponder, to see the beauty, to imagine the world as a peaceful place.

An Extraverted Authentic Blue

My needs and values:

Relationships with family and close friends are the most important and stimulating aspect of my life. As a new grandmother, I am fascinated by the developing personality and the relationship that I have with two little people. I think about how they are unique and what they need from us in order to flourish and not be stifled.

Although I know I must allow them to move away emotionally and physically, I still find my connection with my own children essential and consuming. Close friendships have always been terribly important to me, not necessarily as resources that I need on a day to day basis that must be nurtured by daily contact, but rather as long term, caring relationships that are mutually trusting and respectful.

Meaningful and empathetic relationships bring me joy. I don't like superficiality and I don't like conflict. Ethics are important.

Work also pleases me. I don't have to lead. I am happy to be "sous-chef"! I enjoy a task, a project, and the feeling of accomplishment that comes from achievement.

My strengths:

I love big picture ideas and the stimulation of discussing/exploring these with others. So, for example, it's a delight to be part of a book club that is intimate and is focused on discussions that involve the personal, human relationships and the dynamics of fate and life.

I feel I am quite an intuitive person. Listening, understanding gestures and stories and what is not said as well as what is said, tells me a great deal. I enjoy meeting people, engaging with them brings joy. I enjoy the challenge of welcoming people and trying to help them to feel comfortable enough to share themselves. If people are troubled, they quite often seem to be comfortable talking to me and I feel interested and involved. It is wonderful to be able to help and it makes my own perspective on life broader.

I have loved helping others. For example, when I was young I taught skiing and it was thrilling to share something I loved with people who wanted to learn. We had laughs and it was such fun to see others acquire a skill that brought them pleasure and I had given that to them.

As a librarian, what I enjoyed most was the interaction with patrons, helping them find the material they needed and exploring it with them. The technical side did not particularly interest me.

My potential challenges:

I am probably overly sensitive to criticism, although I like to think that I'm introspective and curious enough that I can accept suggestions from someone I respect. And yes, at times I feel I'm very self-critical.

I tend to get enthusiastic and have been accused of overstatement. But I'm only expressing my reactions honestly.

I recognize that it's important to leave others to their work and decisions. However, this is sometimes not my natural inclination and I have to resist the temptation to jump in and help.

Impact of extroversion on my Temperament:

As an extrovert, I am energized by being with other people and can tend to act first and then reflect. However, I enjoy listening and drawing others out.

I do not learn best by operating in a vacuum. Rather, I am most comfortable talking things through, either on a one-on-one basis, or in large groups.

I enjoy being in situations where I meet new people such as at parties, and I find that I often have very interesting conversations with the people that I meet. Part of what I enjoyed about being a librarian was meeting and talking with new people.

Others have told me that I exude a sense of energy and enthusiasm. I can get very charged by life especially when I am starting a new project or talking to people that I enjoy.

Authentic Blues At Work

The Authentic Blue Leader

Authentic Blues do make great leaders. However, they rarely choose to be in the forefront of political or organizational activity.[36] Rather, they tend to make dynamic leaders by playing the role of mentors, change agents, or advocates.

What Authentic Blue leaders bring to the role is a real commitment to the people who work with them and for them.[37] They use their intuitive ability and sensitivity to identify each individual's true potential both for current positions and future ones. The Authentic Blue leader is at their best when performing a coaching or mentoring role. They have the patience and willingness to work with each individual to help them to develop their strengths in a way that will allow them to contribute to the overall goals of the organization. They motivate and encourage others by giving positive recognition for both working towards and achieving goals. They will often work with their employees to help them find new career opportunities and will continue to mentor them long after they have moved on to other positions.

The Authentic Blue leadership style is participative; they tend to develop a team-based environment where individuals work towards consensus on key issues. They like to create a comfortable atmosphere where people feel safe to share their thoughts and feelings and listen to those of others. Once consensus has been reached, Authentic Blues will likely give employees leeway regarding how they reach their goals. They do not have a tendency to micromanage, preferring not to get involved in the details of how to accomplish the task.

Because of their ability to see the big picture and their gift with words, they are able to inspire others by creating a vision. Authentic Blues can bring together different pieces of information and have an overall sense of what is happening; as a result, they can often see a desired direction for the organization. They can be charismatic in using words, metaphors, stories, and symbols to paint a picture of a desired future that others want to achieve.

Authentic Blue leaders can make a significant contribution during times of change. If they need to implement an organizational change they will spend time identifying how to communicate the change in such a way that they get "buy-in" and commitment. They will also be sensitive to the needs of their employees, and will bring the employees' perspective to the table as the organization plans and implements the change. They will spend the time needed to address individual concerns during times of change – helping employees adapt to and accept change as best they can.

Because Authentic Blues tend to shy away from conflict they of all the Temperaments will find it most difficult to deal with an employee who is not performing well. They may have a tendency to put their head in the sand initially hoping that the person will improve by himself or herself. If this does not work Authentic Blues will spend considerable time and energy coaching the employee to improve. As a last resort they will discipline an employee, however, they may find this very stressful.

A non-cooperative or tension-filled environment can also be stressful for the Authentic Blue Leader. For example, if hard-headed negotiations are required they can perform them, however, they may not feel comfortable doing so.

As leaders, Authentic Blues have to be careful not to "burn out" just because they are so attuned to their employees. They are willing to take the time to listen to both the professional and personal concerns of their employees as they feel comfortable in the counselling role. However, this may give them less time to focus on organizational priorities or their own personal and family lives.

Tips for Working for an Authentic Blue Leader

- Keep to the niceties of communication, for example, "Hi, how are you today?"
- Focus on the big picture
- Don't get bogged down in details when you explain information to the Authentic Blue Leader
- When presenting ideas use more of a humanistic approach rather than a facts and data approach
- Explain how your approach will positively impact on people or fit in with their values or the values of the organization
- Be imaginative in your presentation of ideas
- Focus on the future and not the past
- Use personal examples to make your point
- Don't try to be manipulative, be authentic
- Be willing to dialogue
- Realize that relationships are important
- Make use of stories, metaphors, and analogies when explaining yourself
- Demonstrate that you are actively listening to what your leader is saying

The Authentic Blue Employee

The Authentic Blue employee prefers to work in an environment that is positive and creative where they are able to interact with their co-workers not only from a business perspective but also from a personal one. They like to get to know their co-workers and understand who they are as a whole; their backgrounds, families, likes and dislikes, interests, and abilities. They often form relationships with their co-workers, managers, customers, and anyone with whom they have ongoing contact. People tend to find Authentic Blues easy to talk to, good listeners, and safe to confide in. They need to work in an environment where it is possible to have these interactions. If Authentic Blues find themselves working in an environment where this is not allowed due to the culture of the organization, unrealistic deadlines, strict supervision, or solitary tasks the Authentic Blue may become lonely and stressed.

Authentic Blues are often able to give feedback in a way that is constructive and supportive, allowing others to grow and develop. They also need to receive the same kind of feedback. Without constructive feedback Authentic Blues can often assume the worst, which can cause them to become anxious and doubt their abilities. They consider constructive feedback crucial to the emotional well-being of both themselves and others.

Genuineness is very important to Authentic Blues and they prefer to be honest with others. However, the emotional well-being of all parties is even more important. As a result Authentic Blues will do anything necessary to avoid inflicting emotional pain, even to the extent of not being totally honest, as long as it does not involve going against their moral values. To the Authentic Blue honesty means dealing with others fairly and not manipulating them in any way. They tend to be very cautious of people who they believe are not treating them in an honest manner. However, they do not appreciate brutal honesty and would prefer that others be honest with them in a constructive manner.

Authentic Blues can be very supportive of change in the organization if they think that it is meaningful and in the best interests of the people involved.[38] Because of their sensitivity to the needs of others, they can be helpful in identifying how people are responding to change and what needs to be put in place to help them embrace the new direction. If support is not provided Authentic Blues may become frustrated or angry, act out, or emotionally disengage from the organization.

They may not thrive in situations where a strong attention to detail and the "here and now" is required. They prefer to think in global terms and leave the detail orientation to others. If required, Authentic Blues can focus on details. However, they find it very stressful to do so. Because they are generally thinking about the future rather than the present or past, they may not be at their best when they constantly need to focus on what is happening in the present or on practical realities.

Because of their creativity and affinity for relationships Authentic Blues can often be very productive and inspiring team members. They can help to keep the team motivated, provide emotional support to team mates especially when the going gets tough, and come up with creative and inventive solutions to problems often faced by the team.

Authentic Blues are often effective speakers and writers and they have a creative and artistic flair. They enjoy having the opportunity to express themselves in creative ways. This can lead to a career in the arts, entertainment, media, or creative marketing.

Because of their people orientation Authentic Blues are also drawn to service oriented, teaching, healing, or helping professions. In these professions they can use their skills of seeing the big picture and being empathetic, caring, and intuitive to help people grow and develop. However, because of their aversion to intense competition and conflict they will tend to shy away from professions where they must constantly deal with irate customers or where they are in competition with their co-workers.

Tips for Managing an Authentic Blue Employee

- Treat them with respect
- Attend to their relationship needs
- Create a positive work environment
- Listen to them when they are upset and let them share their emotions if they feel the need to
- Remember to positively recognize them for a job well done
- Don't micromanage
- Allow them the opportunity to express themselves in creative ways

- When presenting new ideas or tasks start with the big picture and then drill down to the detail if necessary

- Make use of their ability to generate ideas

- When trying to get them to buy into an idea present it from the perspective of the positive impact it will have on people

- Use personal exampless, metaphors, and analogies to illustrate points

- Always be genuine and authentic with them

Authentic Blue Superstars

Oprah Winfrey

Oprah Winfrey, the host of *The Oprah Winfrey Show* is a great example of an Authentic Blue. On her show she is willing to share intimate aspects of her own life in the hope that her own experiences can help others. She has shared details of her weight problems, her childhood abuse, and other aspects of her personal life as a learning tool for others. She demonstrates an ability to connect and empathize with her guests so that they in turn reveal intimate details about their lives that fascinate and help her audiences. Like many Authentic Blues, she tends to be interested in topics related to personal growth, quality of life, and self-improvement. She also tries to inform her viewers about abuses that occur throughout the world, such as child sexual abuse and ways in which some of the side-effects of this type of abuse can be overcome and eliminated.

She demonstrates her altruism and caring for others in many ways. In 1998, she started Oprah's Angel Network, a charity geared to encouraging people all around the world to help underprivileged people. She donates more of her personal income to charity than any other show-business celebrity in America does.

Her vision, willingness to try new things, and her creativity has enabled her to have many successful ventures. Her show has earned several Daytime Emmy awards; she is an academy award nominated actress, publishes a magazine, and is involved in several other philanthropic activities.[39]

Mother Theresa

Mother Theresa is another great example of an Authentic Blue. She was a Roman Catholic nun who founded the Missionaries of Charity in Calcutta, and she worked tirelessly for the poor for over 45 years. She was known for her compassion, love and caring of the poor, sick, and dying. She indicated that she was "called" to leave the safety of the convent and go live among the poor so that she could help them.

Like many Authentic Blues, she had very strong values and refused to compromise those values. She stood up for these values against both church and governmental leaders in India and in the world. For example, she believed that abortion was wrong and was not scared to stand up for these views.

Mother Teresa had a vision of helping the poor and her ability to inspire people with that vision enabled her to expand the Missionaries of Charity's work in India and the rest of the world. For example, in 1982, during the Siege of Beirut, Mother Teresa rescued 37 children trapped in a front line hospital by negotiating a temporary cease-fire between the Israeli army and Palestinian guerrillas. She and her helpers also ministered to the hungry in Ethiopia, helped radiation victims in Chernobyl, and assisted earthquake victims in Armenia. At the time of her death, she had developed 610 Missions in 123 countries.[40]

Jimmy Carter

Jimmy Carter, who served as the thirty-ninth President of the United States from 1977 to 1981, was an Authentic Blue who chose to be in the forefront of political activity. However, his Authentic Blue personality really shone through after he left the presidency. Since opening the Carter Center in 1982, he has shown his altruism and deep concern for others by developing many programs to alleviate suffering and improve lives around the world. Examples of his work at the center include conflict resolution, election monitoring, and the promotion of human rights and democracy. He has further demonstrated his idealism and selflessness by working with Habitat for Humanity, an organization devoted to building low-cost housing for the poor.

Jimmy Carter is a deeply spiritual and religious man. He has indicated that Jesus Christ has been the driving force in his life. Even when he was president he prayed several times during the day. He has also served as a Sunday school teacher for most of his life.

Because of his excellent communication skills, his global perspective, and his ability to mediate in conflict situations he has also acted as an elder statesman for various presidents. For example, in 1994, he helped the Clinton administration arrange a nuclear freeze with North Korean Dictator Kim IL Sung and he negotiated a cease-fire between warring Bosnian Muslims and Serbs in Yugoslavia.

In 2002, President Carter received the Nobel Peace Prize for his efforts in finding peaceful solutions to international conflicts, for working on democracy and human rights, and always trying to improve economic and social development.[41]

Section 3

The 4 Temperaments and Stress

Linda Berens points out that Temperament related stress is not the same as the stress that we experience as a result of day-to-day living.[42]   Our work, our relationships, our habits, finances, etc. can cause this type of stress. When our core needs and values are not being met we experience Temperament related stress. Because we are often unaware of how our Temperament causes us stress, we can suffer more than we need to. However, once we understand how our Temperament causes us stress we can find ways to prevent this kind of stress from occurring and to manage it once it has occurred.

6

What Causes Stress?

What Causes Introverts and Extraverts Stress?

Before we discuss what causes stress for the different Temperaments let's first take a look at what causes stress for introverts and extraverts. Earlier we explained the difference between introversion and extraversion. We also discussed how different an extraverted Temperament could be from an introverted one. The same holds true for what stresses out the Temperaments. What causes stress for an introvert can be very different from what causes stress for an extravert no matter what Temperament they are.

Introverts tend to like things to be quieter than extraverts. If it is too noisy this can cause stress for an introvert. On the other hand, if it is too quiet this can be stressful for an extravert.

Extraverts like to work with others. If they find themselves in situations where they are isolated or working virtually alone for long periods of time this can be stressful. Alternatively, introverts would be quite happy working on their own.

Other situations that extraverts can find stressful are having to sit through long meetings, lack of action, and lack of feedback. However, introverts can find it stressful when they have to lead discussions and/ or give large group presentations. Many introverts truly have a greater fear of public speaking than they do of dying.

Finally, some extraverts stress out when they don't receive clear instructions or communications. On the other hand, introverts can find constant supervision and too much time "outside themselves" to be great causes of stress in their lives.[43]

What Causes an Inquiring Green Stress?

As we said earlier, Inquiring Greens are all about the facts and just the facts, so anything to do with emotions is potentially stressful for them.[44] They are not comfortable if others start talking about their emotions and they don't like being in situations where they have to deal with the feelings and emotional development of others. They have no problem with debate or even confrontational situations as long as the discussion remains logical and they can deal with the facts and data surrounding a situation. However, if the discussion becomes emotional Inquiring Greens can find it uncomfortable and stressful.

Inquiring Greens are not interested in small talk so they can become annoyed if they have to engage in mindless chitchat with people. Purely social gatherings, such as cocktail parties, can be stressful for them unless they can find someone with whom they can have a more cerebral conversation.

Incompetence can be another stressor for Inquiring Greens.[45] They pride themselves on their competence and they have difficulty dealing with situations where they don't feel totally competent or they believe other people are incompetent. In these situations, they can become very critical of themselves and others.

They can also find it stressful when other people are too dependent on them or are unable to make decisions. Inquiring Greens are often very independent, decisive people who believe other people should be too. They can also become stressed if they have to work within or respond to another person's agenda too closely or for too long. They like to be in control of any situation in which they are involved. They do not deal well with authoritarian leaders.

Finally, Inquiring Greens can become stressed if they find themselves in situations that are very detail oriented, rigid, and routine. If confronted with too much detail it can be overwhelming to them. They can also find it quite stressful if they don't have a challenge or an opportunity to learn. They need to have the flexibility to do things their own way and once they have figured something out they are ready to move on to something new.

What the Stressed Out Inquiring Green Looks Like

Inquiring Greens tend to internalize a lot of their pressure. This can lead to physical sensations such as stomach aches, headaches, or back pain. When there it too much stress in their lives they can become quite short-tempered, impatient, and frustrated. They can appear quite cold and unfeeling to those around them, often using sarcasm to express their feelings. At times Inquiring Greens can be perceived as insensitive to the feelings others. On occasion, they can become quite angry and enraged, blowing up and losing control. This can be very distressing to an Inquiring Green as they pride themselves on being calm, cool, and collected. If this happens they can become quite self-critical.[46]

Too much detailed information can be overwhelming and/or immobilizing to Inquiring Greens. It may manifest itself in dysfunctional behaviour such as making errors or doing things more slowly.

Under extreme stress they may isolate themselves from situations and people – which can increase their distress. Introverted Inquiring Greens especially can be prone to withdrawing into their own inner world. Once they have isolated themselves they may find it difficult to reconnect with the real world.

Ways an Inquiring Green can Overcome Stress

Greens can do a variety of different things to reduce their stress level. If they have isolated themselves they might find it useful to reconnect with the important people and activities in their lives. Because of their tendency to be overly self critical they may need to take the time to reflect on their successes and achievements or work on projects that confirm their competence and knowledge. If they are suffering from "analysis paralysis" they might find it useful to develop priorities and an action plan so that they can move out of their stuck spot. Even when they are juggling many priorities taking on a new project will help energize them and reduce the stress that they are experiencing.

The other Temperaments can help Inquiring Greens alleviate their stress. Because dealing with emotional reactions is never easy for an Inquiring Green, Authentic Blues can help them understand

and come to terms with these emotions.[47]   They can help Inquiring Greens understand what they are feeling, why they are feeling that way, and how their behaviour is affecting others. As Inquiring Greens can get caught up in their own world when under stress, Organized Golds can bring them back to reality by helping them refocus on their responsibilities and commitments. Inquiring Greens can become so focused on becoming knowledgeable and being competent that they may forget to have fun. Resourceful Oranges can help them enjoy themselves and not take things so seriously. They can also help Inquiring Greens toughen up and get back into the action if they have isolated themselves.

What Causes a Resourceful Orange Stress?

Resourceful Orange's happy go lucky approach to life often enables them to handle stress better than the other Temperaments. However, there are still things that can stress them. They do not function well in environments where there are rigidly enforced rules and procedures, schedules or a lack of flexibility in how to do things.[48]   Often at the top of their list of what causes them stress is being micromanaged. When micromanaged they may feel claustrophobic as though they don't have enough room to do the task in a way that makes sense to them. Feeling used and unappreciated can also cause stress for Resourceful Oranges. They work hard and need positive recognition for their contribution.

Routine and boredom can also be major stressors.[49]   Resourceful Oranges hate having to do the same tasks repeatedly. Physical activity is also very important for a Resourceful Orange. If forced to sit still for too long in endless meetings and presentations,they can become quite agitated.

What the Stressed Out Resourceful Orange Looks Like

Stressed out Resourceful Oranges can become confrontational and aggressive with others. Under duress, they can lash out at people at work, home or in life generally. They can get into trouble when they rebel against issues that frustrate them. When extremely stressed they may express their anger in a physical manner.

Another behaviour that they may exhibit when stressed out is procrastination, avoiding or putting off what they should be doing. However, as they generally need to be busy, they may just do meaningless work or goof off and find something fun to do instead. When stressed, they can break rules and take risks that have negative consequences for themselves and others. Because Resourceful Oranges do not believe in rules just for the sake of rules they may break them if they do not see a reason for them or feel constrained by them. They may also engage in risky behaviour such as not coming to work on time, leaving early, taking days off, or missing deadlines.

When extremely stressed, some Resourceful Oranges may resort to stimulants or engage in other addictive behaviours.[50] This gives them a false sense of well being in the moment and they may find these quick fixes hard to eliminate.

It is not often that a Resourceful Orange will experience physical symptoms related to stress. However, if they do it will usually manifest itself in the form of memory or appetite loss.

Ways a Resourceful Orange can Overcome Stress

When stressed out, Resourceful Oranges may need to use their creativity and ingenuity to find different ways to bring spontaneity, freedom, fun, and excitement back into their life. They will need to make sure that these options are not harmful.

A new challenge can also re-energize the Resourceful Orange. At work, this may take the form of applying for a more challenging job or a demanding project where they can use their skills and get the recognition that they need. In their personal lives it could be taking up a new hobby such as playing an instrument or making jewelry. Physical activity can provide a great stress release for Resourceful Oranges. They may be wise to incorporate sports into their lives as they tend to be the most physical of all the Temperaments. A physical release helps to relieve their psychological stress.

The other Temperaments can help the Resourceful Orange when they are under stress.[51] Authentic Blues will try to understand the behaviour of stressed-out Resourceful Oranges and work with them to develop different coping mechanisms. Organized Golds will guide them to manage their time, make a plan and follow through on it, or help them understand why it is important to stick to the rules. The Inquiring Greens will challenge them to look at the big picture and not get bogged down in the details of day-to-day life.

What Causes an Organized Gold Stress?

High standards are important to Organized Golds for both themselves and others. These standards can lead to a great deal of stress and guilt as they often feel they are not doing enough or just can't seem to get it right.

Organized Golds dislike disorganization. If they find themselves in a situation that is not going according to plan, or worse yet there is no plan, they can become very agitated. Emergencies are not comfortable for them as actions need to be taken on a moment-by-moment basis and most Organized Golds don't tend to live in the moment. They like to have time to plan what is going to happen.

As stated earlier, change is not an Organized Gold's friend. They like to know what they are supposed to do and when they are supposed to do it by. Organized Gold's embrace tradition, and as such, often relate what they are doing today to their past experiences. They are most comfortable when they are doing something which is familiar to them. As a result, when they find themselves in situations where there is frequent change they can feel very lost and anxious.

Introverted Organized Golds may find it very stressful when they need to interact with many new people because they cannot draw on their past relationships with them as a way of knowing how to communicate and get along.

Because Organized Golds are natural planners and will go out of their way to ensure the completion of a plan; they are not as comfortable with spontaneity. For example, on the weekend they like to know what they will be doing and accomplishing each day. They often have lists that spell out what they will be doing, where they will be going, who they will be seeing, what they need to take with them, etc. If a friend were to call them last minute and say "I am feeling a little tired today. Do you mind if we go to a movie instead of going to the museum this afternoon?" they might find this stressful because it is not what they had planned. It would not be unusual for an Organized Gold who is sick to keep a social engagement because they made a commitment, and fell it is very important to honour it.

Organized Golds don't like to wait around for anything. Whether it is standing in line at the grocery store or waiting for others to come to a decision they can find this stressful as they see it as a waste of time. In the grocery store situation, they believe the store should have planned for busier times and had enough cashiers available so that customers did not have to wait. Regarding making a decision, they don't like to spend time ruminating over possible alternatives. They believe that once viable options are presented a decision should be reached and then acted upon.

A vacation, which many of us think of as a time to unwind, relax, recharge, and get away from our day-to-day lives, may actually be very stressful experience for an Organized Gold. This is because of their strong sense of responsibility. They never believe they can be away from the office for any length of time because many people depend on them to get things done and keep things running smoothly. While on vacation they will often worry about what kind of mess they will return to and how much work will be required to get things back on track. In addition, they don't believe in just taking time to rest while on vacation. They believe they should do something productive like immersing themselves in the culture they are experiencing, or completing projects at home. As a result they may spend so much of their vacation actually working that they don't take any time to rest and relax. Consequently they can actually return home more tired than when they left.

A surprise party is probably not something to arrange for an Organized Gold. They can find surprises very uncomfortable and usually don't enjoy them. This goes back to their need to plan and be prepared at all times. They may also feel that they are not appropriately dressed for the occasion or that they have not had the opportunity to prepare their speech to thank people for being there. Overall, the occasion would probably be stressful for an Organized Gold and have the opposite effect of being a pleasant surprise for them.

Finally, an Organized Gold can find it very difficult when there is any conflict amongst their family, friends, or their co-workers. To an Organized Gold it is very important to maintain order in their lives and the lives of those around them. They are the caretakers in society, so if they find themselves in a situation where there is disorder they will work to rectify the problem. In the process, they may overtax themselves or become overwhelmed by the situation.

What the Stressed Out Organized Gold Looks Like

When an Organized Gold is stressed it can present itself in a number of different ways. Sometimes their need to be prepared makes them think of all the possible negative outcomes in any possible situation. They can then feel very tense and/or depressed. Some Organized Golds may present themselves as being very quiet, calm, and sombre on the outside as a way of hiding their tension and depression on the inside. At other times they may become quite irritable because they feel totally overwhelmed by everything they believe they are responsible for.

Organized Golds can have a stubborn streak which is even more pronounced when they are under stress. They will often exhibit a very assertive or authoritarian attitude, taking on a "my way or the highway" approach to life.

Stress can exhibit itself in the form of both physical and mental symptoms.[52] From a physical perspective many Organized Golds experience a sense of fatigue and/or muscle tension. Some Organized Golds have also reported that when stressed they are much more likely to over eat or crave the wrong foods. From a mental perspective, they will often experience a feeling of irritability, a temporary loss of memory, an inability to think clearly or even momentary feelings of panic. Very stressed Organized Golds may begin procrastinating.

Ways an Organized Gold can Overcome Stress

One of the best ways an Organized Gold can overcome, or better yet avoid, stress is to know when to ask for help. They tend to take on too much work because they feel a sense of responsibility or believe a job will not get done if they don't do it. They don't like to admit they need help because they always want to appear competent. However, it is a crucial step in avoiding burnout. They must also learn how to say "No" so that they do not become overloaded with too much to do.

Organized Golds can also benefit from learning how to relax; they should research different relaxation techniques such as meditation, yoga or other approaches that have well documented success. Techniques that encourage Organized Golds to focus the activity and not the ever-present "to do" list in their mind are great stress relievers.

It is impossible to be prepared for all situations and to always be in familiar surroundings. Organized Golds may benefit from taking preparedness classes such as: CPR/first aid, winter driver training and parenting; so as to feel more comfortable with the unexpected.

In times of change Organized Golds need to draw on past experiences and reflect on changes that went well; they need to figure out a process and time line for dealing with the change. Organized Golds should seek out input from others who have gone through similar changes to ask advice on what they can anticipate. This can be achieved by looking at topical internet forums or speaking one-on-one with friends and family members. While each change process is unique, this research gives them an idea of what they can anticipate.

Finally, Organized Golds need the help of the other Temperaments to help them handle their stress, as each in their own way can help to balance out the Organized Gold.[53] The fun loving, spontaneous, Resourceful Oranges can drive the Organized Golds crazy but their sense of play can help to counter-balance an Organized Gold's "all work no play" attitude towards life. The Authentic Blues can offer the Organized Golds sympathy when they are feeling hard done by for all of the work they have to do. They can also offer inspiration that can lift the heart of an overwhelmed, anxious Organized Gold. Finally, the Inquiring Greens know when to question the Organized Golds if they focus too much on what they have done in the past and are not willing to look at alternate possibilities when making decisions.

What Causes an Authentic Blue Stress?

As stated earlier, Authentic Blues do not like conflict and they can find it quite stressful. They can even experience stress if they believe that a situation might lead to conflict. Working in hostile, critical, or confrontational environments can be highly stressful for them. Criticisms or even being in a position where they are being evaluated or having to evaluate others can also be very stressful.

Guilt is a major factor in the life of an Authentic Blue and it can cause them to feel quite stressed. They can experience guilt over anything from fearing they have offended a co-worker when the co-worker does not say "good morning" to having to leave early because they have a sick child at home.

Authentic Blues are innovative and creative and they embrace meaningful change. If they find themselves in a work environment which does not allow for innovation or which is very structured or scheduled this can lead to stress. It can be stressful for an Authentic Blue if they have to perform the same routine tasks on a daily basis, or the work is repetitive and mindless.

Finally, relationships, people, and values are important to Authentic Blues. Therefore, if their work environment is impersonal or inauthentic they will not be happy and ultimately this will lead to stress. Equally, they will find it hard to work in situations where they believe people are being exploited or treated unfairly. They can experience stress if they have to deal with people who they believe are hypocritical or insincere.

What the Stressed Out Authentic Blue Looks Like

One of the first signs that an Authentic Blue is stressed is they often become very quiet and withdrawn and may even seem remote. Even the introverted Authentic Blues tend to become quieter than usual. They may also become more rigid and some become very busy. If they are pushed too far Authentic Blues can become quite short tempered, impatient, irritable, moody, and even sarcastic. They can become out of control and burst out with angry, hurtful emotions. Afterwards they may feel guilty about their outburst which actually causes them more stress.

Because they tend to take things to heart, stressed out Authentic Blues often over personalize things, become defensive, self-critical, and feel inadequate. They can sometimes wallow in self-pity. They can become very pessimistic even to the point of anticipating and experiencing all of the negative possibilities.

Because of their relationship focus, two other behaviours are typical of the stressed-out Authentic Blue. First, to avoid their own problems they may become overly involved in helping other people, to the extent that they rescue rather than help the person. Second, at the best of times, Authentic Blues find it hard to say "No", and when stressed out they can find it almost impossible.[54] At work, this can add to their stress as they may agree to take on too much and further burden themselves.

Stress can take a physical and mental toll on Authentic Blues. They often suffer physical symptoms such as sleep disturbances, headaches, stomach problems, and overeating. This can result in physical illness and they may have to take time off from work. From a psychological perspective they can become depressed, obsessive-compulsive, impatient, disorganized, and overlook and forget details even more than they normally do.

Ways an Authentic Blue can Overcome Stress

First and foremost, Authentic Blues need to learn how to take care of themselves – both emotionally and physically. This may be hard for them as they have a tendency to ignore themselves and take care of others. In times of stress, they might need to re-examine what gives them a sense of purpose and find new ways to provide themselves with meaning in their life.

They may also need to learn how to say "No". This does not come easily to Authentic Blues, as they believe in helping others. However, it is a major source of burn out for them. They need to decide what is most important to them in life and set priorities accordingly. This will help them determine when they can say "No".

Authentic Blues need to rationally deal with their feelings of guilt.

They need to recognize they may experience guilt when they have no reason to feel that way. For example, they forgot to ask a co-worker how their weekend was and the co-worker was not at all upset about this. They also need to recognize that feeling guilty is a trap that they can easily fall into and they must recognize and stop this self-defeating behaviour before it causes them harm.

If they find themselves in a job that does not meet their Temperament needs, for example, it does not give them an opportunity to use creative or innovative thinking or develop authentic relationships, they may need to look elsewhere.

The other Temperaments can be of assistance in alleviating stress for the Authentic Blues.[55] The Inquiring Greens can bring a calm rationality to any situation. They can help Authentic Blues set clear boundaries so that the people in their lives do not over burden them. The Organized Golds can bring more stability and organization into their lives by helping them to achieve a stronger grasp of some of the practical realities. Last, but certainly not least, the Resourceful Oranges can bring a sense of play and more lightheartedness into their lives. They can also help Authentic Blues become more emotionally resilient.

Overcoming Stress Activity

Take a few minutes to think about yourself when you are stressed.

What causes you stress?

What do you look like when under stress?

What techniques will help you manage your stress? (Going for a walk, talking with a friend over a cup of tea, etc.)

Section 4

The ABC's of Reading and Communicating with People at Work

One of the most important skills that we bring to the workplace is the ability to understand people and communicate effectively with them. While everyone is unique, we can gain valuable insight into our co-workers' personalities by identifying if they are introverted or extraverted and what their Temperaments are. Once we have determined an individual's introversion/extraversion preference as well as their Temperament, we can analyze how best to communicate with and influence them. As you read the following information keep in mind that we are presenting generalizations. Not everyone will fit the general pattern for introversion/extraversion or each Temperament.

7

How to Read Other People

How to Read Introverts and Extraverts

As we discussed in chapter 1, an additional element, while not a formal part of Temperament theory, is still very important, that is the difference between introversion and extraversion.

The following chart will help you to read whether a person is an introvert or an extravert.

Extraverts	Introverts
Tends to think out loud	Tends to think inside their head
Expresses thoughts and feelings	Keeps thoughts and feelings to themselves
Tends to act first and then reflect	Tends to reflect and then act
Prefers to problem solve by talking it through with others	Prefers to problem solving by working it through on their own
Seen as outgoing	Seen as quiet
Has a broad circle of friends	Has an intimate circle of friends
Tends to be energized after a day of working with others	Tends to be energized after a day of working on their own
Has many interests	Explores a few interests in depth
Tends to project a sense of enthusiasm and energy	Tends to project a sense of calmness and tranquility
Tends to demonstrate more animated body language	Tends to demonstrate less animated body language

How to Read an Inquiring Green

You will be able to identify an Inquiring Green because they focus on the big picture, concepts and abstract information rather than the specifics. They tend to be logical and objective and they like to talk about systems and principles. When explaining their thinking they will present a series of logical statements followed by a logical conclusion. You will find that they tend to talk about the future rather than the present.[56]

Appearance – The way they look

Inquiring Greens will present differently based on whether they are introverts or extraverts. Introverts can be so focused on their inner world that appearance is not necessarily important to them. They may not even be aware of the way they look. An example of this would be Albert Einstein who tended to look dishevelled, for example, his hair always looked wild and unkempt. Extraverts on the other hand tend to take great pride in the way that they appear to the world because they believe it demonstrates their success. To illustrate their success some wear designer clothes, live in lavish homes, and drive expensive cars.

Body Language – The way they move

Demonstrating a calm, collected demeanour is important to Inquiring Greens. Outwardly they often attempt to show that they are rational and in control of themselves. As a rule, they will not use excessive arm gestures or body movements. Their face will generally not show emotion because they try to keep their emotions under tight control. Their tone of voice will tend to be neutral. In an effort to demonstrate their self control they may at times come across as arrogant and cold.

This cool demeanour may break down if they become highly stressed. Then they may loose their cool and become very tense, sarcastic, or irritable.

Communication – The words they use

Inquiring Greens usually have large vocabularies and they tend to use precise language. Because their thinking style is complex, they can use rather long drawn out sentences that might be confusing to others. In an effort to explain complex ideas, they are fond of using models and schematic diagrams as a clarification technique. Analogies and metaphors are favoured tools used to make their points. They also like to play with words. You will often know you are dealing with an Inquiring Green if they use a lot of puns, complex terms, and double meanings.

When writing they tend to present their points logically and systematically. However, their choice of complex sentence structures and words can sometimes makes their writing difficult to understand.

Disposition – The way they present themselves

Inquiring Greens generally present themselves as competent people who are confident in their own abilities. Usually they like to associate with people who are well respected and they tend to distance themselves from people that they don't hold in high esteem. At times they can come across as arrogant or dismissive because of their high self-regard. Of all the Temperaments, they are the best at debating with and critiquing the ideas of others. As a matter of fact they often enjoy taking on the role of devil's advocate.

Passions and pastimes

Many Inquiring Greens believe their career is all important. As a consequence they many spend long hours at work strategising how they can get ahead. Because of this focus on work other parts of their life such as family and friends can sometimes be neglected.
Self improvement is another great passion for them. They like to take courses, study on the internet, listen to tapes, or read books to increase their knowledge. They often enjoy learning a new language, studying the ancient Greeks, or learning how to use a new computer application.

For their hobbies, they like to focus on those areas where they can challenge themselves and apply their knowledge, skill, and strategic thinking. Games like monopoly, chess, and dungeons and dragons are very appealing. Sports such as golf or skiing can also be attractive to them. Many Inquiring Greens have an innate ability with computers and the introverted Inquiring Greens may spend a great deal of time on their computer.

How to Read a Resourceful Orange

You will be able to identify a Resourceful Orange by their down to earth practical approach to life. They are more inclined to focus on life's details rather than the big picture. They also like to live life to its fullest; they are happy with a last minute change of plans and embrace change wholeheartedly. To a Resourceful Orange life is an experience and it is meant to be lived in the here and now. Their motto is "embrace today, the past is the past, can't change it so why rehash it, and who knows what the future may hold".

Appearance – The way they look

Resourceful Oranges embrace casual Fridays. You will notice that they like to be dressed in a comfortable manner that allows them room to move.[57]   To some of the other Temperaments they may even appear a little too relaxed, for example, preferring to carry a knapsack instead of a brief case as it is much more practical and comfortable to carry. However, they are very aware of the details; you are not likely to see a Resourceful Orange with a missing button or a safety pin holding things together. They like to look good but in an easygoing way. They tend to have a love of accessories especially the ones that are more unusual or fun.

Body Language – The way they move

A bit like a humming bird, the Resourceful Orange's body tends to move at a constant, fast pace. However, because of their acute sense of body awareness they often appear to be very graceful. They are very comfortable within their own skin. However, they often like to have something to play with such as a pen or small change. When bored they can become very fidgety because of their need for movement.

Communication – The words they use

As with everything else they do in life, the Resourceful Orange tends to have a very casual, uncomplicated communication style. Their sentence structure tends to be free flowing; they are usually up on the latest slang and are comfortable making use of it. Resourceful Oranges don't like to hang around or waste time in anything they do and this can even be noticeable in the way they speak. They tend to make use of contractions and sometimes leave off the final letter or sound of words. For example, instead of saying "I have got to pick up some milk on the way home" you might here them say "I've gotta get milk on the way home". When explaining something they will tend to make use of real life experiences, either their own or those of others. It is not unusual to hear a Resourceful Orange make use of a sports metaphor to put explanations in terms that are easy to understand.

Disposition – The way they present themselves

Relaxed is really the best way to describe a Resourceful Orange. They are probably the easiest Temperament to be around because of their easy going, uncomplicated, and happy approach to life. They live in the present and are usually very much aware of what is going on around them. They are always ready to respond no matter what the situation. If you find yourself in a crisis a Resourceful Orange is the person you want to have around as they tend to be cool headed and don't get frazzled by whatever is thrown at them.

Passions and pastimes

If it involves movement, whether it be of the whole body or just working with their hands, the Resourceful Orange will be there. Most love to either play or at least be involved in sports of some kind. Resourceful Oranges are often referred to as adrenaline junkies and tend to be attracted to the more extreme sports such as skydiving, car racing, or ski jumping. They also like to play games and usually the more active the better. For example, a Resourceful Orange is more likely to enjoy a game of twister than they are a game of scrabble.

Resourceful Oranges are often very adept at using tools and because of this they are often attracted to hobbies such as home renovations, metal working, or gardening. They enjoy anything that involves making use of their hands and tools.

How to Read an Organized Gold

Organized Golds tend to focus on facts, data, and specifics. They are essentially practical in their approach and not prone to flights of fancy. They live in the moment rather than in the future. If you work with an Organized Gold you will notice that they are prepared and efficient.[58] They generally excel at planning and organizing and they are very comfortable working with rules, standards, and procedures. They are punctual and expect others to be the same.

Appearance – The way they look

Traditional and appropriate would be the way to describe how Organized Golds present themselves to the world. They are not slaves to fashion and would prefer to present themselves as neat, well-dressed people who do not stand out in a crowd. Generally, they will have clean, well styled hair and neat, coordinated clothes and shoes. Their overall presentation is of someone who is put together. Practicality is very important to them and they would generally prefer to have something that is comfortable rather than stylish.

Body Language – The way they move

Their body language reflects their pragmatic, matter of fact approach to life. Unlike some Temperaments, they don't tend to be expressive or flamboyant. Rather, their body movements are measured and deliberate. As a rule they have good eye contact with others. Generally their tone of voice is well modulated and clear so that others can understand their message. Reflecting their purposeful approach to life they usually have good posture and tend to walk briskly. They strongly believe in social appropriateness and will keep to the niceties of greeting people, saying goodbye, etc.

Communication – The words they use

The words that they use tend to reflect the practical, no nonsense type of people they are. They will use clear, easily understood words to get across their message. They tend to relate information to their own past experience. For example, they might say "From my experience..." or "In the past..." They usually present information in a logical, sequential way, focusing on facts and details. It is important to them that the words that they use are politically correct and polite.

Extraverted Organized Golds may be quite talkative however, their conversation tends to focus on facts, details, and information.

Their written style tends to be clear, logical and to the point, outlining the necessary information in detail. Some of the other Temperaments may find it a little too detailed for their taste.

Disposition – The way they present themselves

Organized Golds tend to come across as responsible, serious people who do what they say they are going to do. As a general rule, they believe in hierarchy, rules, standards and procedures and they work effectively within this kind of structure. Unfailingly cooperative, they are always willing to help to get the job done. They believe in common sense and usually demonstrate it through their actions. Belonging is important to them and they like to be included in work and social activities. They tend to prefer routine and they don't always like to change from the way that things have always been done. Indeed, they often have "shoulds" and "ought to's" about how things should be done.

Passions and pastimes

Organized Golds enjoy belonging to groups and they believe in contributing time and energy to their community. Often pillars of their society, they tend to do volunteer work for their religious organization, local hospital, or service organization. If they are parents, they are frequently on the parent-teacher association; they volunteer for cubs or brownies or manage one of their children's sport teams. At work they meet their social needs and their desire to contribute by volunteering to work on social clubs, etc. They have many different hobbies. Some enjoy activities where they can be physical such as; sports, gardening, hiking, or bird watching. Others enjoy using their hands to do arts and crafts such as knitting, embroidery, pottery, or carpentry.

How to Read an Authentic Blue

Appearance – The way they look

Because they value being unique and original Authentic Blues don't often show too much uniformity in how they dress.[59]   However, as they like to be unique, they often wear clothes, jewelry, shoes, or accessories that make a statement about who they are. The Authentic Blues that are more free-flowing will have fun with clothes. They might like to wear funky clothes and accessories that express who they are – acquiring bits and pieces at vintage stores, boutiques, or from their great grandmother.

Other Authentic Blues tend to be a little more conventional – especially those that work in organizations. They will have a tendency to wear clothes that are suitable for their environment and they will definitely have a more coordinated look. However, they will still try to find ways to express who they genuinely are as human beings by making use of unique accessories.

Body language – The way they move

The body language of Authentic Blues may differ depending on whether they are introverts or extraverts. Extraverts tend to be very expressive, using flowing arm gestures, body movement, and facial expressions to convey their ideas. They often express themselves very passionately when talking about something they believe in. Generally, they will convey warmth by smiling or leaning in towards the other person to show that they are listening. Alternately introverted Authentic Blues may hang back initially and come across as a little distant until they feel comfortable in a situation.

At times, they are so caught up in their own world of concepts and ideas that they can appear slightly clumsy. As a result, they may bump into a table or trip over a briefcase.

Communication – The words they use

Authentic Blues can be very articulate – especially when they are talking about concepts or people. Making an impact on others is important to them so they often use expressive words like "amazing" or "wonderful". They prefer to use global language and convey general impressions rather than specific data. In fact, they can find it difficult to give precise information such as directions on how to get to a specific location, or a detailed description of an event that had occurred. They are gifted at using metaphors, analogies, and personal experiences as a way of ensuring that others understand their point of view.

Like their verbal communication, their writing tends to be flowing and colourful. They will use global, dramatic language to express themselves and may tend to be wordier than other Temperaments.

Disposition – The way they present themselves

As a rule, they tend to present themselves as the warm, nurturing people they are. They are masters at listening and giving empathy to others – especially when talking about personal issues. Extraverted Authentic Blues are not scared of revealing personal information about themselves or asking others questions that reveal personal information.

Authentic Blues can become engrossed in conversations that focus on personal issues, self-development, their values, or helping others. While introverted Authentic Blues will only have these conversations with people they know well, extraverted Authentic Blues can meet people at cocktail parties or on planes and have very intimate conversations about their lives.

They are most comfortable when talking at the global level and because they see connections between ideas that others do not see as easily they may appear to jump from one idea to another.

Because they can be lost in their world of thoughts others may perceive them as detached from reality and perhaps a little dreamy.

Passions and pastimes

People and relationships are very important to Authentic Blues and they love to engage in meaningful conversations with others where they can be truly authentic.

Personal growth is a passion for Authentic Blues. They enjoy reading self-help books, attending courses or talking to others who can help them grow as individuals.

Authentic Blues are often dedicated to helping others or to causes that will help humanity. On a micro level, they are willing to help friends, associates, and clients by coaching and supporting them. They are often energized by helping others grow and reach their full potential. On a macro level, some Authentic Blues will dedicate themselves to world issues such as literacy, hunger, etc.

They are naturally creative with thoughts, ideas, and words and enjoy thinking outside of the box or engaging in creative activities such as writing or drama.

Authentic Blues can be deeply spiritual. Their spiritual path may be traditional or not as they are attracted to different paths.

Communicating Effectively with the Different Temperaments

Here are some suggestions on how to communicate effectively with people of other Temperaments.[60]

Inquiring Green	
General Approach	<ul><li>Be logical and rational in your approach</li><li>Know your facts and don't bluff</li><li>Talk about concepts and patterns rather than specific details</li><li>Acknowledge their expertise and competence</li></ul>
How to Influence Them	<ul><li>Present the big picture first</li><li>They will be persuaded by logic, objectivity and a coherent argument</li><li>Expect to be challenged and critiqued and don't take it personally</li><li>Use diagrams and models to explain your ideas</li><li>To engage them, define the end goal and allow them to problem solve</li><li>Be prepared to explain the rationale behind your ideas</li><li>Give them time to work through your arguments</li></ul>
Words to Use	<ul><li>Use logical, precise language</li><li>They enjoy complex ideas and words</li><li>Don't bore them with too much practical detail</li><li>Use metaphors and analogies to clarify your ideas</li></ul>
Body Language	<ul><li>Present yourself in a confident way</li><li>Don't use overly demonstrative body language</li><li>Maintain a calm exterior even if things do not go your way</li><li>Don't get flustered by their cool or arrogant approach to you</li></ul>

Resourceful Orange

General Approach	<ul><li>Be open and relaxed in your approach</li><li>Keep things moving – Resourceful Oranges can get bored if the pace or processes are moving slowly</li><li>Give them information they can use right away</li></ul>
How to Influence them	<ul><li>Keep the information practical and tangible</li><li>Present things in an action-oriented manner</li><li>Talk about what is current and happening now, they are not interested in the past or the future</li><li>Explain how your approach will impact things immediately or in the very near future</li><li>Don't talk for too long</li><li>If possible use a demonstration and get them physically involved</li><li>Make it fun</li></ul>
Words to Use	<ul><li>Make use of jargon, colloquialisms, and slang</li><li>Keep concise and to the point, don't use a lot of ten dollar words</li><li>Use action oriented graphic words to paint a picture</li><li>Don't just use words – use actions as well to demonstrate what you are saying</li><li>Make use of sports metaphors (i.e., Is everyone ready for the big game today? – when asking if the team is ready for the presentation they are making to the clients)</li><li>Make use of humour to keep it light and upbeat. You can even be somewhat outrageous</li></ul>
Body Language	<ul><li>Keep moving</li><li>Demonstrate rather than tell, where possible</li><li>Laugh along with them</li></ul>

Organized Gold

General Approach	<ul><li>Be practical in your approach</li><li>Draw on the past</li><li>Be organized and practical</li><li>Give background information and lots of supporting data</li><li>Keep on track</li><li>Dress appropriately – pay attention to detail (i.e., make sure your nails are clean, hair brushed, shirt tucked in)</li></ul>
How to Influence Them	<ul><li>Present the information in an organized manner – start small and work your way up to the big picture</li><li>Explain how your approach will positively impact the bottom line or save time and energy</li><li>Use examples from the past to illustrate points</li><li>Focus on the past and today – how it can be done more efficiently</li><li>Talk about the process and how it worked effectively in the past</li><li>Clearly define roles and responsibilities</li><li>Keep your presentation simple, concentrating on the detailed data and how it will improve the process</li><li>Talk in terms or protocol and defined processes</li><li>Speak in a clear and concise manner</li><li>Take a position of authority</li></ul>
Words to Use	<ul><li>Use traditional language</li><li>Be well mannered</li><li>Put things into quantifiable terms</li><li>Compare and contrast things (i.e. "We had better success with this approach than that one.")</li><li>Make use of rating scales</li><li>Explain rather than demonstrate</li></ul>
Body Language	<ul><li>Don't be overly expressive</li><li>Demonstrate authority through your body language</li><li>Present yourself in a calm, respectful manner</li></ul>

Authentic Blue	
General Approach	• Be friendly and warm in your approach by keeping to the niceties of communication, (i.e., "Hi, how are you today?") • Be sincere • Listen carefully to what they have to say – they often have great insights about issues and people • Show empathy and a desire to build a real relationship
How to Influence Them	• Present the big picture first • Explain how your approach will positively impact on people or fit into the values of your listener • Use personal examples to illustrate points • Focus on the future and possibilities· You can be imaginative in your presentation of ideas • Don't bog them down with details • Engage them in a dialogue • Ask them for their thoughts and feeling on the matter
Words to Use	• Use global language and concepts • Metaphors, analogies, and stories can be used to explain your point of view • Don't bore them with too much practical detail
Body Language	• Smile • Demonstrate warmth through your body language • Use your hands to emphasize points • Lean slightly into the speaker to demonstrate that you are listening

Section 5

The 4 Temperaments and Finding the Right Career Fit For You

There are a number of ways that the career chapters can help you. You may be just starting out and want to find a rewarding career, or you may have been downsized and want to take time to re-evaluate what is the right "fit" for you, or you may feel burnt-out in your existing career and in need of a change. Whatever the case, it is time well spent to focus on finding a career that is fulfilling. The right career choice will greatly increase your chances of long-term career success, satisfaction, and overall happiness. Wouldn't it be wonderful if you could work in a job that constantly interests, stimulates, and challenges you, rather than one where you are reluctant to go to work each morning?

Understanding your Temperament can go a long way towards helping you find your right career choice. In the following four chapters, we will focus on each Temperament as it relates to potential career choices. In each chapter, we will summarize the needs, values, strengths, and challenges of each Temperament. Then we will outline the different careers that many people with that preference have found appealing. You will find that some careers appear in more than one Temperament list – that is because we are all "plaid" and have abilities that enable us to do many different jobs.

Although you will receive a lot of valuable information in each chapter, we would also recommend that you work with a Career Counselling Practitioner. A practitioner can help you further clarify your career path with additional assessments that look at other aspects such as your interests, aptitudes, and achievements.

As you read through the chapter for your predominant Temperament, remember to keep in mind whether you are an introvert or extravert, as that will play a part in the careers to which you are drawn. Once you have completed the chapter and identified careers that are of interest to you, fill out the "Understanding Yourself Activity".

If you have not already determined your predominant Temperament you will need to complete the assessment in Chapter 1. If you found your top two scores in chapter 1 were close you may want to read through the chapters for both Temperaments.

8

Inquiring Green Careers

Needs and Values

- Becoming competent and being seen as competent by others is important to you.

- You have an ongoing quest for knowledge and you want to understand the way things (not people) work and why.

- Logical reasoning is high on your list of values; you pride yourself on your logical thought patterns and enjoy listening to new ideas as long as they use correct reasoning.

- You are an independent thinker and place a high value on achievement and intelligence.

- You strive to achieve your goals and set high standards for yourself and you expect others to do the same.

- Your chosen career is often the place where you strive to achieve results, as being successful is important to you.

- You do not like to be told what to do or how you should think – it is important to you to make your own decisions.

- You may be drawn to scientific inquiry and enjoy logical investigation, reasoning, and the universal laws behind science.

- You value progress and improvement; you are oriented to the future and progression.

- You use knowledge to gain improvement in the way things are done.

Strengths

- You are a great problem solver and are especially adept at dealing with complex issues.

- You attack and resolve problems by using your exceptional powers of concentration and vast knowledge of conceptual models.

- You tend to be a big picture thinker and like to focus on improving the way systems work.

- You often embrace change and are an effective change agent.

- You can be a visionary leader and will find ways to keep things moving forward.

- You prefer to be involved at the start of project when you can suggest creative ideas and ways for the whole system to move forward.

- You bring a healthy scepticism to everything in which you are involved.

- Often you are able to logically analyze the situation and by making use of your healthy scepticism you are able to find the flaw in the logic or the missing link.

- When you do find a flaw you are not scared to voice your opinions and fight for what you believe is right.

- You don't believe in bringing emotion into a reasoned argument.

- If someone finds a genuine flaw in your logic or theory you appreciate the feedback.

- You like to read, research, and gather information and can really focus when something is important to you.

- You prefer to stay cool, calm and in control of yourself in a crisis; you will work hard to present a calm exterior.

- You are often clever and witty with words and love games, riddles, mental tricks and repartee.

- You enjoy showing your mental powers by solving complex intellectual exercises.

Potential Challenges

- You sometimes seem to be insensitive to the feelings of others and as a result others can see you as cold and uncaring.

- You can be impatient and show a lack of understanding towards people who use emotional arguments or pleas.

- Because detailed information makes sense to you at the big picture level you may have difficulty explaining the details to others.

- At times, you can become impatient with others and seem irritable and even arrogant.

- You dislike repetitive or illogical arguments, redundancy in any form and incompetence and will either withdraw or make comments that will show your impatience.

- You can suffer from information overload because you are always acquiring new information about subjects that interest you.

- You can be indecisive in the face of too much information and this can lead to analysis paralysis and a lack of follow through on your part.

- You are self-critical and can sometimes feel inadequate when you don't know enough, can't comprehend a situation, or you don't measure up to your own high standards.

- At times, you may be out of touch with what is happening around you.

- Because you sometimes get lost in your own thoughts you don't always keep to social conventions.

Understanding Yourself Activity

Based on the summary above, answer the following questions:

What values are important to you?

What are your strengths?

What are your challenges?

Work Preferences for an Inquiring Green

The following lists contain jobs that have attracted people who have identified themselves as Inquiring Greens. Please note, however, that you are not limited to the list for your particular Temperament. We all have a range of skills that enable us to do many different jobs. In addition, these lists offer just a sampling of jobs that each Temperament would find rewarding.[61]

As you read through the lists check those that you would like to explore in greater detail.

Business, Consulting and Finance

When it comes to the world of business, consulting and finance, Inquiring Greens tend to desire positions of leadership, authority, and control. These positions require them to do things such as map out the best course of action to take or to develop contingency plans. It also enables them to make use of their long-range thinking and strong analytical abilities. These positions additionally allow them to make use of their abilities to forecast trends and design imaginative ways to take advantage of opportunities for themselves and their clients. Inquiring Greens also enjoy making money and working with other people's money. They prefer projects that are large-scale because they are big-picture thinkers. These projects also allow them to work with powerful and influential people.[62] Inquiring Greens tend to be able to take charge of situations in a quick and efficient manner. That, combined with their ability to stick to the facts when making decisions, allows them to make tough decisions fairly. This also allows them to set organizational policy without getting bogged down in the people side of issues. As long as they are able to delegate the details to competent staff they will often be happy and do well in these positions:

- ❏ Accountant
- ❏ Administrator: Explore all categories
- ❏ Auditor
- ❏ Business General: Self-employed
- ❏ Consultant: Explore all categories
- ❏ Corporate Vision Consultant
- ❏ Credit Investigator or Mortgage Broker
- ❏ Industrial / Labour Relations
- ❏ Insurance Agent, Broker, or Underwriter
- ❏ Manager: Corporate, Financial, Sales, Hospitality, or Engineering
- ❏ Human Resources
- ❏ Project Manager
- ❏ Real Estate Agent or Broker
- ❏ Sales Representative
- ❏ Stockbroker
- ❏ Strategic Planner

Health Care

Inquiring Greens often enjoy health care because it can be cutting-edge and they can continue to learn new knowledge and skills. They are frequently drawn to the highly complex technical areas of medicine. Introverted Inquiring Greens especially are attracted to these areas because they can often work alone with minimal outside input. Additionally these areas usually attract other intellectually gifted people who Inquiring Greens tend to find stimulating.[63]   Finally, medicine allows them to make use of their excellent reasoning skills.

- ❐ Acupuncturist
- ❐ Biomedical Engineer or Researcher
- ❐ Doctor: Explore all categories
- ❐ Hypnotherapy
- ❐ Laboratory Technologist or Technician
- ❐ Medical Assistant or Technician
- ❐ Medical Researcher
- ❐ Nuclear Medicine Technologist
- ❐ Nursing: Consultant / Educator
- ❐ Occupational Therapist
- ❐ Pharmacist
- ❐ Psychodrama Therapist
- ❐ Psychologist or Counsellor
- ❐ Scientist
- ❐ Speech Pathologist
- ❐ Veterinarian or Vet Technician

Education, Training and Coaching

Inquiring Greens are drawn to education, training, and coaching because it allows them to continue to explore and consider new and different approaches. They usually prefer to teach at the college or university level. In general, they prefer to work with the more advanced and challenging programs and students. These programs allow them to focus on the big picture and conduct research in and teach complex systems and theories. Extraverted Inquiring Greens in particular can be excellent and stimulating trainers. They use their creative design abilities to develop a challenging, structured, and interactive learning environment.[64]

- ❏ Career Development Practitioner
- ❏ Coach: Executive, Life Skills, or Athletics
- ❏ Debate Teacher / Coach
- ❏ Education: Explore All Categories
- ❏ Organizational Developer
- ❏ Philosopher
- ❏ Researcher
- ❏ School Principal
- ❏ Teacher: Explore all categories
- ❏ Theorist
- ❏ Professor: College / University

Public Service, Government, Politics and Law

This is an area that tends to attract extraverted Inquiring Greens as they are drawn to people with power and like working with a variety of different people. They also can be excellent public speakers, because they make use of figurative, expansive language, and express great vision. It allows them to make use of their ideas, knowledge, and personal wisdom in a fast paced and powerful arena. Additionally, they are able to use their abilities to see trends, themes, and shifts in public opinion and react quickly to them.[65]

- ❏ City Works Technician
- ❏ Corrections Officer or Probation Officer
- ❏ Criminologist

- ❏ Forensics
- ❏ Lawyer, Attorney, Judge
- ❏ Legal Secretary or Assistant
- ❏ Manager: City, County, Provincial/State Government
- ❏ Military Officer or Enlistee
- ❏ Paralegal or Legal Research
- ❏ Political Analyst or Advisor
- ❏ Politician
- ❏ Social Services Worker

Creative Endeavours (Arts, Entertainment, Marketing and Communications)

Inquiring Greens are drawn to creative endeavours because of their ability and need to do unique work. Inventors create new systems or devices that make improvements to the current way of doing things or solve life's annoying problems. Writers and artists make use of their big picture perspective to create new and exciting works. The fields of marketing, advertising, and public relations allow Inquiring Greens to develop and execute their ideas in creative and engaging ways. The extraverts enjoy public relations and advertising because it is fast-paced and glamorous. Additionally, it allows them to use their ability to spot trends. Finally, it satisfies their never ending curiousity and active imagination.[66]

- ❏ Actor, Entertainer
- ❏ Advertising
- ❏ Architect
- ❏ Art Advisor or Art Critic
- ❏ Artist, Sculptor, Illustrator
- ❏ Comedy Writer, Comedian
- ❏ Composer, Lyricist
- ❏ Editor
- ❏ Farmer

- ❏ Grant Proposal Writer
- ❏ Graphic Design Artist
- ❏ Industrial Designer
- ❏ Inventor
- ❏ Journalist, Reporter, Columnist
- ❏ Marketing
- ❏ Media /Public Relations Specialist
- ❏ Movie Critic
- ❏ Musician
- ❏ On-line Multimedia Content Developer
- ❏ Photographer
- ❏ Playwright
- ❏ Producer / Director: Movie, Radio, TV, Video
- ❏ Publicity Writer
- ❏ Publisher
- ❏ Radio / TV Broadcaster
- ❏ Speech Writer
- ❏ Writer: Explore all categories

Technology, Science and Technical

Inquiring Greens are drawn to technology, science and technical fields for many reasons. These fields allow them to analyze problems and develop creative solutions. They can also make use of their ability to understand complex problems and find ways to eliminate errors or vulnerabilities. Using their big-picture thinking they easily see how systems, products, or services fit within the context of the whole company, industry, or technology.[67] These fields offer them the opportunity to work with high-tech equipment and products that are rapidly changing and expanding.

- ❏ Aerospace Worker
- ❏ Anthropologist

- ❏ Archaeologist
- ❏ Astronomer
- ❏ Astrophysicist
- ❏ Auto CAD Technician
- ❏ Chemical Technician
- ❏ Chemist
- ❏ Computer Work: Explore all categories
- ❏ Ecologist
- ❏ Electrician
- ❏ Electronic Sales Representative
- ❏ Electronic or Electrical Technician
- ❏ Engineer: Explore all categories
- ❏ Environmental Worker
- ❏ Factory Worker, Site Supervisor
- ❏ Geologist
- ❏ Geophysicist
- ❏ Marine Biologist
- ❏ Mathematics
- ❏ Mechanic: Explore all categories
- ❏ Oceanographer
- ❏ Pilot
- ❏ Social Scientist
- ❏ Software Programmer
- ❏ Surveyor
- ❏ Technician or Technologist: Explore all categories

Inquiring Green Final Activity

What are the top ten careers that you would like to explore in greater depth?

1.

2.

3.

4.

5.

6.

7.

8.

9.

10.

Both Canada and the United States have a number of web sites that you can use to explore careers in greater depth. Two that we would recommend are:

In Canada:
http://www.jobfutures.ca/en/home.shtml

In the USA:
www.jobbankinfo.org/

9

Resourceful Orange Careers

Needs and Values

- You want the freedom to express yourself in whatever way you choose – at work, with your family, or in your leisure time.

- You highly value excitement and action.

- Spontaneity is important to you.

- Variety is the spice of life and you thrive on change and unpredictability.

- You dislike boredom and in these situations you like to stir things up a little so that it is more interesting.

- You want to become highly proficient and recognized in your chosen endeavour.

- You prize flexibility and adaptability.

- Making an impact is very important to you – if you can't do it in a positive way, then you may do it by shocking or defying society.

- Being challenged and taking risks is energizing for you.

- You live in the moment and believe in enjoying yourself and having a good time.

Strengths

- Adaptability is one of your key strengths as you are able to respond flexibly to new circumstances and crisis situations.

- You are willing to take risks and act – even if there is an element of danger.

- Perfecting your ability to become a skillful performer in your chosen area of interest is something you will work tirelessly at.

- You are gifted in and enjoy using tools – whether it is a hammer, a computer, or words.

- You have a "hands on" learning style and learn effectively from watching, being shown what to do, and then doing it.

- You're masterful at negotiation and promotion.

- You are persuasive and quick on your feet.

- You can perform effectively under pressure.

- Tactically gifted, you use your senses to scan the environment, assess what is happening, and choose the most successful course of action.

- You're an effective practical problem solver and trouble shooter.

- You are realistic and focus on what works best.

- You can think creatively to come up with a variety of potential solutions to the problem at hand.

- You're a generous and fun-loving team participant.

- You often take a light hearted attitude towards life.

- You're known as the world's optimist, you usually see the cup as half full rather than half empty.

Potential Challenges

- You need your freedom, and can become bored easily.

- Because of your dislike for routine work, you can seem unpredictable and unprepared.

- While you enjoy jumping into new activities, you may find it difficult to complete them – especially if you no longer perceive them as interesting.

- Others may see you as irresponsible when you do not follow through on agreed upon actions.

- Sometimes you can act too quickly before truly understanding the big picture and the long term consequences of your actions.

- Unnecessary rules and regulations frustrate you and you may bend or break them when they don't make sense.

- As a natural risk-taker and adventurer, you can sometimes expose yourself to unnecessary risks.

- If you do not find a place to fit in you can become unhappy, unfulfilled, and start to buck the system.

- If you can't get the adrenalin rush through normal activities, there is a potential to try other methods.

Understanding Yourself Activity

Based on the summary above, answer the following questions:

What values are important to you?

What are your strengths?

What are your challenges?

Work Preferences for a Resourceful Orange

The following lists contain jobs that have attracted people who have identified themselves as Resourceful Orange. Please note, however, that you are not limited to the list for your particular Temperament. We all have a range of skills that enable us to do many different jobs. In addition, these lists offer just a sampling of jobs that each Temperament would find rewarding.[68]

As you read through the lists check those that you would like to explore in greater detail.

Business and Finance

Resourceful Oranges are attracted to business and finance positions that give them the opportunity to work in a fast-paced environment where there is variety and freedom. They don't tend to be interested in business or finance positions where there are defined rules and routines that have to be followed. Their willingness to take risks and act quickly attracts them to positions such as investment trading or real estate. They love the adrenalin rush attached to taking a risk on the stock market or working on the sale of a house. Their pragmatism and detail orientation also allows them to be successful in other finance careers such as banking as long as they can work in an environment that gives them autonomy and freedom.[69] Entrepreneurial in nature they often open up their own businesses. They love the creativity and excitement of setting up a new business and trying to make it work. They also enjoy the autonomy and variety that occurs in entrepreneurial ventures.

- ❐ Auctioneer
- ❐ Banking
- ❐ Car Sales
- ❐ Cashier
- ❐ Clerical Worker
- ❐ Credit Investigator
- ❐ Economist
- ❐ Entrepreneurs: Explore all categories
- ❐ Executive or Administrative Assistant
- ❐ Investment Trader

- ❒ Insurance Agent or Broker
- ❒ Insurance Underwriter
- ❒ Mortgage Broker
- ❒ Negotiator: sales or contracts
- ❒ Office Manager
- ❒ Personal Assistant
- ❒ Real Estate Broker
- ❒ Sales Representative/Manager
- ❒ Self-employed Business
- ❒ Stockbroker
- ❒ Storekeeper

Action and Sports

Occupations that are filled with action and excitement are very appealing to Resourceful Oranges. Many of these jobs require the effective use of tools and they work hard to perfect their skills in this area. Resourceful Oranges hate routine and flourish in jobs where there is variety. A job such as firefighter or police officer is appealing because every day has the potential to be completely different. Their adaptability and ability to respond to crisis situations also makes them well suited to these types of jobs. Because they enjoy using their bodies and perfecting their technique, they are often attracted to the field of professional sports. They will practice tirelessly to prefect their ability to kick a ball, take a golf shot, or jump over a hurdle. They are also drawn to jobs involved in sport's leadership such as athletic coaching.

- ❒ Adventure Trainer
- ❒ Athletic Coach
- ❒ Dancer
- ❒ Dance Instructor
- ❒ Firefighter
- ❒ Flight Attendant

- ❏ Helicopter Pilot
- ❏ Jockey
- ❏ Lifeguard
- ❏ Military: Officer or Enlistee
- ❏ Park Ranger
- ❏ Pilot
- ❏ Police Officer
- ❏ Private Investigator
- ❏ Professional athlete: Explore all categories
- ❏ Race Car Driver
- ❏ Secret Service Agent
- ❏ Security
- ❏ Sports Administrator
- ❏ Stunt Person

Entertainment

Some Resourceful Oranges are attracted to the world of entertainment. For them, it appeals to their love of entertaining and amusing others.[70] They enjoy public performance because they can demonstrate mastery of their art. They also enjoy the adrenalin rush that comes from performing in front of others. In these professions they are rarely bored because there is variety and freedom from routine. Many of these jobs require that they are adaptable and flexible and respond in the moment to whatever is happening. They love to have fun themselves and they bring humour, wit, and energy to the world of entertainment.

- ❏ Acting Coach
- ❏ Actor
- ❏ Broadcaster
- ❏ Broadcasting Technician
- ❏ Cartoonist
- ❏ Comedian
- ❏ Comedy Writer

- ❏ Cruise Director
- ❏ Director of Movies, Radio or TV
- ❏ Disc Jockey
- ❏ Entertainer
- ❏ Journalist, Reporter
- ❏ Magician
- ❏ Media/Public Relations Specialist
- ❏ Mime artist
- ❏ Musician
- ❏ Performing Artist: Explore all categories
- ❏ Producer
- ❏ Public speaker
- ❏ Writer

Trades

These jobs frequently attract Resourceful Oranges because they enjoy using tools and will work tirelessly to perfect their ability with their chosen tool. The tool may be a bulldozer, a tractor, a skill saw, or a sewing machine. Most of these jobs involve movement and action that appeals to the Resourceful Orange personality. They tend to be interested in how things work and as they are great practical problem solvers they enjoy the challenge of mending a broken tool or thinking through the best way to mend a leaking sink.

Independent by nature, they thrive in careers like farming and construction where they can usually call their own shots. Because some Resourceful Oranges are energized by excitement and unpredictability, they can enjoy careers like cooking where they frequently have to work to tight deadlines.

- ❏ Audiovisual Specialist
- ❏ Bartending
- ❏ Carpenter
- ❏ Chef, Cook

- ❐ Cosmetologist
- ❐ Cabinetmaker
- ❐ Dressmaker or Tailor
- ❐ Electrician
- ❐ Farmer
- ❐ Hairdresser
- ❐ Heavy Equipment Operator
- ❐ Landscape Architect
- ❐ Maintenance worker
- ❐ Mechanic
- ❐ Plumber
- ❐ Painter
- ❐ School Bus Driver
- ❐ Steelworker
- ❐ Surveyor
- ❐ Truck Driver
- ❐ Transportation Operator
- ❐ Warehouse, Freight, and Other Labours

Technical

As Resourceful Oranges like to use their hands and are interested in how things work and function they can have career satisfaction in technical positions.[71] They will take the time to master the tools, techniques, and machines involved in their position. Because focusing on specifics and practical problem solving is something they enjoy, working in a position such as computer programming is of interest to them. Some of these positions require that they work under pressure and Resourceful Oranges thrive in these situations.

- ❐ Air Traffic Controller
- ❐ Architectural Technician
- ❐ City Works Technician

- ❑ Computer Programmer
- ❑ Construction Estimator
- ❑ Drafting Technologist
- ❑ Engineer: Explore all categories
- ❑ Industrial Instrument Technician
- ❑ Marine Biologist
- ❑ Mechanical Engineering Technician
- ❑ Network Engineer
- ❑ Quality Assurance Technician
- ❑ Sound Technician
- ❑ Surveyor
- ❑ Technician: Explore all categories
- ❑ Technical Trainer
- ❑ Telecommunications Specialist
- ❑ User Support Technician

Health Care

Some Resourceful Oranges enjoy working in health care. There are two types of positions that they are generally drawn to – those where they can respond to an emergency or those where they can use tools and machines effectively. They will often flourish in positions such as a paramedic or emergency room doctor because they have the ability to think calmly and respond appropriately in emergencies.[72] In addition, the variety of the job and the movement inherent in these positions brings out the best in Resourceful Oranges. They also flourish in positions such as a laboratory technologist or an optometrist where they can work skillfully with tools and machines to complete their tasks.

- ❑ Audiologist
- ❑ Chiropractor
- ❑ Crisis Centre Worker

- ❑ Dental Hygienists and Assistants
- ❑ Dietician Nutritionist
- ❑ Doctor: Explore all categories
- ❑ Emergency Technicians
- ❑ Hearing Aid Dispenser
- ❑ Hospital worker: Explore all categories
- ❑ Laboratory Technologist
- ❑ Massage Therapist
- ❑ Medical Assistant
- ❑ Nursing
- ❑ Optometrist/Optician
- ❑ Paramedic
- ❑ Pharmacist
- ❑ Physical Therapist or Technician
- ❑ Radiology Technician
- ❑ Rehab Specialist
- ❑ Respiratory Therapist
- ❑ Veterinary Assistant
- ❑ Visiting Nurse
- ❑ X-ray Technician

Arts and Crafts

Careers in the world of arts and crafts suit many Resourceful Oranges because of their creativity. They will work hard to perfect their technique and become a skillful performer in their chosen field whether it is painting, potting, illustrating, or sculpting. Indeed once working on something they like, they can work tirelessly through the night to finish it. Most of these jobs give them opportunities to work on their own with minimal supervision – which appeals to their sense of freedom. They enjoy detail work and this preference is well used in jobs such as jewelry design or illustrating. Because they are willing to take risks they will put all of their energies into a career such as sculpting or photojournalism even though they know it can be hard to make a living from these occupations.

- ❐ Art Buyer
- ❐ Artist
- ❐ Art Gallery Worker
- ❐ Craft Worker
- ❐ Fashion Designer or Illustrator
- ❐ Fashion Stylist
- ❐ Florist
- ❐ Graphic Designer
- ❐ Illustrator
- ❐ Interior Decorator
- ❐ Interior Design
- ❐ Jewelry Designer
- ❐ Painter
- ❐ Photo Journalist
- ❐ Potter
- ❐ Set Designer
- ❐ Sculpture
- ❐ Textile Designer

Resourceful Orange Final Activity

What are the top ten careers that you would like to explore?

1.

2.

3.

4.

5.

6.

7.

8.

9.

10.

Both Canada and the United States have a number of web sites that you can use to explore careers in greater depth. Two that we would recommend are:

In Canada:
http://www.jobfutures.ca/en/home.shtml

In the USA:
www.jobbankinfo.org/

10

Organized Gold Careers

Needs and Values

- You need to feel a sense of belonging to your family, work, and social group.

- You value tradition.

- Safety and security are important values because you know that life is unpredictable and it is important to plan for potential challenges.

- You take on the role of protector for those that you feel responsible for.

- Duty and responsibility are key and you believe that if everyone contributes their fair share then the world will be a more stable and equitable place.

- You believe in solid leadership and hierarchical structures within organizations where everyone clearly knows who they report to and what their duties are.

- You value organization and planning.

- You believe in commitment and follow-through.

- You pride yourself on being prepared and saving for a rainy day.

- You have a need for positive recognition and appreciate it when others recognize you.

Strengths

- You have excellent planning and organizing skills.

- Time management is one of your key strengths.

- You will work conscientiously to achieve your plan.

- You take pride in your punctuality.

- As an Organized Gold, you use sound judgment (often reflecting on your past experience) and logical thinking based on the facts of the situation.

- Others would describe you as having a lot of common sense.

- You have a keen attention to detail.

- Dependable, hard working and reliable would be how others describe you.

- You believe in excellence and have high standards for yourselves and others.

- You can review highly detailed work, identify errors and correct them.

- Once you have noticed mistakes in others' work, you are competent at giving feedback.

- You always do what you say you are going to do.

- Because belonging is important to you, you strive to be a cooperative and willing team member.

- You provide cultural stability by maintaining the traditions of your family and community.

- You work tirelessly for any group to which you belong.

Potential Challenges

- Because you believe in maintaining high standards, you can be critical and authoritative.

- You can be overly respectful of those in authority.

- You can become resentful and bitter if you do not receive enough recognition for the work that you do.

- From your perspective the world is an unstable place, and because of this you often live in a constant state of anxiety.

- You can take a very pessimistic view of life.

- Always trying to do your best and being responsible can cause you to become overworked and exhausted.

- You can be resistant to change.

- You may focus too much on the past and maintain traditions even when they are no longer relevant.

- You may have difficulty seeing the big picture because you are too focused on specifics.

Understanding Yourself Activity

Based on the summary above answer the following questions:

What values are important to you?

What are your strengths?

What are your challenges?

Work Preferences for an Organized Gold

The following lists contain jobs that have attracted Organized Golds. Please note, however, that you are not limited to the list for your particular Temperament. We all have a range of abilities that enable us to do many different jobs. In addition, these lists offer just a sampling of jobs that each Temperament would find rewarding.[73]

As you read through the lists check those that you would like to explore in greater detail.

Business and Administration

Because of their logical thinking ability and their attention to detail Organized Golds are often attracted to careers in business and administration. They are highly competent as administrators because they like to follow an established set of procedures and are detail oriented and well organized. Some Organized Golds have a natural ability with numbers and they pride themselves on their accuracy and their ability to remember facts and details. They are comfortable in organizations such as banks and insurance companies that are hierarchical in nature and have defined traditions. Because they clearly define roles and responsibilities, plan, and organize work and delegate effectively they often make effective supervisors and managers.[74]

- ❒ Accountant
- ❒ Auditor
- ❒ Banking
- ❒ Bookkeeper
- ❒ Business Management
- ❒ Cashier
- ❒ Chief Financial Officer
- ❒ Claims or Payroll Clerk
- ❒ Clerical Worker
- ❒ Credit Analyst/Counsellor
- ❒ Collection Agent
- ❒ Court Reporter
- ❒ Economist

❑ Executive Assistant

❑ Financial Planner

❑ Insurance

❑ Management and Supervisory Positions

❑ Management Consultant

❑ Project Management

❑ Purchasing Agent

❑ Receptionist, Typist, or Clerical worker

❑ Reservation Manager

❑ Statistical Clerk

❑ Statistician

❑ Telephone Operator

Health Care

Organized Golds are often drawn to medical occupations because of their belief in helping and serving others. Their careful attention to detail and their planning and organizing skills enable them to assess and manage patient care. Practical in nature, they enjoy helping people in a tangible, specific way.[75] They are drawn to hospitals and other medical institutions because they feel comfortable working in hierarchical structures where there are clear lines of authority and accountability. Being part of a large community like a hospital meets their needs for belonging. They are also very comfortable taking on management and leadership positions in medical institutions. Because they are highly responsible and use their planning, organizing, and delegation skills effectively, they often excel in these positions.

❑ Chiropractor

❑ Dental Assistant or Hygienist

❑ Dentist

❑ Dialysis Technician

❑ Dietician

- ☐ Doctor
- ☐ Geriatric Care Worker
- ☐ Geneticist
- ☐ Health Care Administrator
- ☐ Hospital Worker/Manager
- ☐ Medical Assistant
- ☐ Medical Billing Service
- ☐ Nursing
- ☐ Occupational Therapist
- ☐ Optometrist
- ☐ Pharmacist
- ☐ Physiotherapist
- ☐ Radiology or X-ray Technician
- ☐ Speech Pathologist
- ☐ Veterinarian

Education

Educational positions often appeal to Organized Golds because they have high standards and gain satisfaction from imparting knowledge to others and helping them attain the required level of education. They excel when they can teach practical and technical information to their students.[76] Organized Golds are also drawn to educational environments because they believe in doing their duty and being responsible. Educational environments appeal to them because it meets their needs for belonging and they like to work in a defined organizational structure where there are clear roles, responsibilities, and rules. Because of their planning and organizing skills they are often found in management and leadership positions in these institutions.

- ☐ Archivist
- ☐ Child Care Worker

- ☐ Coaching
- ☐ College or Technical/Trade School Instructor
- ☐ Counsellor
- ☐ Corporate Trainer
- ☐ Driving Instructor
- ☐ Guidance Counsellor
- ☐ Principal
- ☐ Teacher: Explore all categories
- ☐ Teacher's Aid
- ☐ School Administrator
- ☐ School Librarian
- ☐ School Bus Driver
- ☐ School Secretary

Government and Law

Government positions often appeal to Organized Golds because they believe in rules, regulations, and maintaining the stability of their community. They have good memories for facts and information and they like to work in a systematic, step-by-step way to perform their tasks. Most of these positions have a clear set of rules and responsibilities that Organized Golds prefer to work within. They also feel comfortable working in a structured, hierarchical environment. Legal positions are often satisfying to Organized Golds. They are very good at remembering facts and details and they can use their specific knowledge of the law to help resolve legal matters. They excel at following set procedures and reviewing document and arguments to identify flaws and inaccuracies.

- ☐ Community Health Worker
- ☐ Court Reporter
- ☐ Government Employee: Explore all categories
- ☐ Judge

- ❑ Lawyer
- ❑ Legal Secretary
- ❑ Legal Researcher
- ❑ Management Positions in Government
- ❑ Military Officer
- ❑ Police or Corrections Officer
- ❑ Probation Officer
- ❑ Postal Clerk

Sales and Service

Organized Golds can find satisfaction in service positions because they believe in doing their duty and helping others in their community. They are practical and use their common sense to make tangible improvements in the lives of others. They are dependable, hard working, and reliable and they will persevere even in difficult circumstances. Some Organized Golds thrive in sales positions – especially when they are selling tangible products.[77] They use their excellent memory for facts to learn the features and benefits of their sales product. They are able to present them to their client in a very logical and factual manner.

- ❑ Caterer
- ❑ Cleaning Service Worker
- ❑ Customer Service Representative
- ❑ Flight Attendant
- ❑ Food Service Worker
- ❑ Fund-raiser
- ❑ Funeral Home Director
- ❑ Geriatric Care Worker
- ❑ Hairdresser or Barber
- ❑ Ministers of Religion
- ❑ Other Religious Positions

- ❏ Private Household Worker
- ❏ Real Estate Agent
- ❏ Sales
- ❏ Social Services Worker
- ❏ Social Worker

Trades

The trades allow Organized Golds to apply their mechanical abilities to concrete, specific assignments. They can use their logical thought process, planning, and organizing skills to work step-by-step through their tasks. They also enjoy using practical problem solving skills to get the job done in a timely fashion and to trouble shoot when problems arise. Many of these professions allow them to work with a certain level of autonomy within a hierarchical structure with clearly defined roles and responsibilities.

- ❏ Carpenter
- ❏ Chef/Cook
- ❏ Contractor
- ❏ Construction Worker
- ❏ Electrician
- ❏ Farmer
- ❏ Machine Operator
- ❏ Machine Fitter
- ❏ Mechanic
- ❏ Painter
- ❏ Plumber
- ❏ Tailor and Dressmaker
- ❏ Telephone Operator
- ❏ Transportation Operator
- ❏ Upholsterer
- ❏ Welder

Technical

Organized Golds are attracted to technical positions because they can use their specific knowledge and expertise to deal with tangible challenges. They like to apply a proven process or procedure to the matter at hand. Because of their precision and accuracy, they are able to follow procedures without making mistakes. Often these procedures are hands on, as in the case of a pilot. Their logical problem solving and decision-making abilities are also an asset in these types of positions. They often enjoy working in traditional organizations where there are clearly defined organizational structures and lines of authority.

❏ Architectural Technician

❏ City Works Technician

❏ Computer Worker

❏ Construction Estimator

❏ Data Base Administrator

❏ Drafting Technologist

❏ Engineer

❏ Forensics

❏ Hardware/Software Tester

❏ Industrial Instrument Technician

❏ Logistics

❏ Mechanical Engineering Technician

❏ Network Administrator

❏ Pilot

❏ Science Technician

❏ Surveyor

❏ Sound Technician

❏ Technician: Explore all categories

❏ Technical Writer

❏ User Support Technician

Organized Gold Final Activity

What are the top ten careers that you would like to explore?

1.

2.

3.

4.

5.

6.

7.

8.

9.

10.

Both Canada and the United States have a number of web sites that you can use to explore careers in greater depth. Two that we would recommend are:

In Canada:
http://www.jobfutures.ca/en/home.shtml

In the USA:
www.jobbankinfo.org/

11

Authentic Blue Careers

Needs and Values

- Self-actualization is important to you, and you are always trying to improve to be the best that you can be.

- You always look for meaning and significance in everything you do.

- You have a strong belief in human potential and helping others to grow and develop is important to you.

- You see yourself as unique and like others to acknowledge your uniqueness.

- Relationships are important to you and they must be empathic and meaningful.

- You prefer to build bridges with others rather than be in conflict with them; ideally, you would like to have a life full of harmony and unity.

- You enjoy working in a synergistic and creative way with others to create better results.

- Your imagination allows you to be innovative in the way you resolve problems.

- You strive to be authentic in all that you do.

Strengths

- Communicating with others is an area where you often excel.

- You are a great team player.

- You are able to persuade others by making use of analogies and metaphors and story telling.

- Because you are an empathetic listener you are frequently able to see the deeper meaning in what others are saying.
- You are attuned not only to the words others use, but also their body language, facial expressions and tone of voice.
- Others feel really heard and understood when they interact with you.
- You are quick to give praise when it is genuinely deserved.
- You are supportive and caring.
- You are able to identify and develop the potential of others.
- Working with others to achieve team goals is enjoyable to you.
- You are a good coach, co-worker, and friend.
- You are intuitive both in individual and group situations.
- You naturally gravitate towards conceptual information and the big picture.
- Because you are future orientated you are often able to see others full potential.
- You are able to look at information from various perspectives and integrate it into a unified theme, frequently seeing patterns and connections that others may not be able to see.

Potential Challenges

- You can be overly sensitive when you are in conflict or receiving negative feedback.
- At times you can be very self-critical if you feel you have failed in some way.
- You are finely attuned to conflict. However, you do not like to deal with it.
- You may tend to avoid or accommodate others rather than confront problems and be in conflict with them.
- You may have a tendency to overstate things.
- Sometimes you may find it difficult to describe things in a detailed manner.

- Because of your ability to see connections and patterns you may make incorrect assumptions based on limited facts.
- You may spend too much time on relationships and not enough on getting the task done.
- You can have difficulty saying "No".

Understanding Yourself Activity

Based on the summary above, answer the following questions:

What values are important to you?

What are your strengths?

What are your challenges?

Work Preferences for Authentic Blues

The following lists contain jobs that have attracted people who have identified themselves as Authentic Blue. Please note, however, that you are not limited to the list for your particular Temperament. We all have a range of skills that enable us to do many different jobs. In addition, these lists offer just a sampling of jobs that each Temperament would find rewarding.[78]

As you read through the lists check those that you would like to explore in greater detail.

Business and Consulting

There are many jobs in the world of business and consulting that appeal to Authentic Blues. Often positions in this field allow them to build relationships and/or work with people to help them grow and develop. Areas such as human resources and organizational development (the people positions in organizations) are ideal for this. They will tend to prefer to work in smaller organizations where they can have the most impact. Furthermore, jobs where they can be independent, but at the same time maintain close relationships with others will attract them.[79] Leadership or executive positions can be appealing because they allow Authentic Blues to work with the big picture. They are also attracted to jobs where they can make use of their creative problem solving skills. Authentic Blues do well in business and consulting as long as they don't have to deal with a lot of conflict or mundane details on a day to day basis.

- ❐ Advertising
- ❐ Career Development Practitioner
- ❐ Change Management Consultant
- ❐ Consultant: Explore all categories
- ❐ Corporate Trainer
- ❐ Employment Interviewer
- ❐ Employment Development Specialist
- ❐ Event Planner
- ❐ Foreign Language Translator
- ❐ Home Management Advisor or Home Economist
- ❐ Home Schooling Consultant
- ❐ Human Resources
- ❐ Instructional Designer
- ❐ International Development
- ❐ International Relations Specialist
- ❐ Insurance Agent, Broker, or Underwriter
- ❐ Market Analyst

- ❏ Marketing Specialist
- ❏ Motivational Speaker
- ❏ Paralegal Executive
- ❏ Property Manager
- ❏ Recruiter
- ❏ Retail Sales Representative, Manager
- ❏ Sales Representative
- ❏ Secretary: Executive or Administrative Assistant
- ❏ Special Needs Consultant
- ❏ Storekeeper
- ❏ Wardrobe/Fashion Consultant
- ❏ Wedding Consultant

Health Care

Authentic Blues are often drawn to medical occupations because they truly care about people. They also love to learn so they are often fascinated by this ever-evolving field. They are open to both western and eastern medicine. Looking at disease from psychological, emotional, and spiritual perspectives, they are drawn to areas where they have the opportunity to work directly with patients.[80] These positions allow them to make use of their relationship-building skills, as well as allowing them to help others grow and develop to overcome health issues. Patients tend to feel at ease with Authentic Blues because they feel listened to and understood. As empathetic listeners they are often able to see the deeper meaning in what the patient is saying. This combined with their ability to interpret nonverbal expression and be intuitive often makes them effective diagnosticians. After diagnosis, their creative problem solving skills kick in to determine the best treatment plan. They tend to treat patients as whole people rather than a set of specific symptoms. Authentic Blues can also be drawn to the administrative side of medicine as they see this as a way to improve patient care.

- ❏ Art Therapist
- ❏ Biologist

- ❏ Chiropractor
- ❏ Dental Assistant/Hygienist
- ❏ Dietician or Nutritionist
- ❏ Doctor: Explore all categories
- ❏ Health Care Provider: Explore all categories
- ❏ Health Technologist or Technician
- ❏ Herbalist
- ❏ Homeopath
- ❏ Hospital Worker/Manger
- ❏ Hypnotherapy
- ❏ Massage Therapist
- ❏ Medical Administration
- ❏ Medical Assistant, Secretary
- ❏ Naturopath or Natural Therapist
- ❏ Nursing
- ❏ Occupational Therapist
- ❏ Palliative Care Worker
- ❏ Pharmacist
- ❏ Pharmacy Assistant
- ❏ Physiotherapist or Technician
- ❏ Psychologist
- ❏ Psychodrama Therapist
- ❏ Public Health Worker
- ❏ Rehabilitation Worker
- ❏ Special Needs Worker
- ❏ Speech Pathologist
- ❏ Therapist
- ❏ Veterinarian or Vet Technician

Service and Hospitality

Service and hospitality positions are often appealing to Authentic Blues because these jobs allow them to combine their love of people with their fascination with growth and development. In all of these careers they interact with people. In many of them, they are helping to make people's lives better. They are also assisting people to add more fun and enjoyment to their lives. This field often offers them the opportunity to see positive results from their efforts, which is very important to Authentic Blues.

- ❏ Advocate
- ❏ Airline Representative
- ❏ Bartender
- ❏ Cashier
- ❏ Chef/Cook
- ❏ Child Care Worker
- ❏ Companion/Seeing Eye Dog Trainer
- ❏ Cosmetologist
- ❏ Family Care Provider
- ❏ Flight Attendant
- ❏ Food Services Worker
- ❏ Hairdresser, Barber
- ❏ Hospitality Worker/Manager
- ❏ Skin Care Specialist
- ❏ Spa/Resort Worker
- ❏ Recreation
- ❏ Tour Guide
- ❏ Travel Agent/Consultant

Education

Authentic Blues are drawn to education because it allows them to help people grow and develop, to reach their full potential. In the process, they are also able to explore and deepen their own understanding of the subject matter. Educational environments are often very cooperative. The atmosphere tends to be harmonious, open to the sharing of ideas and information. This type of setting is very appealing to Authentic Blues. The field of education offers opportunities for both introverted and extraverted Authentic Blues. There are positions such as teaching where extraverts can work directly with people. However, there are also positions where introverted Authentic Blues can work predominately on their own, such as researching. Authentic Blues prefer to work in subject areas that are meaningful and of interest to them. Often they prefer to work with adults rather than children, as adult levels of motivation to learn is often greater. The positions of researchers and librarians are often appealing as these allow for deeper and more meaningful levels of understanding.[81]

- ❐ Administration: Education
- ❐ Adult Educator
- ❐ Aerobics Teacher
- ❐ Early Childhood Educator
- ❐ Education: Explore all categories
- ❐ Librarian
- ❐ Library Attendant
- ❐ Professor: College/University
- ❐ Researcher
- ❐ Research Assistant
- ❐ Teacher: Explore all categories

Social Service, Government and Law

This area attracts Authentic Blues because it allows them to have a positive impact on society and make the world a better place. They are often able to see positive results from their work, which is important to them. It is an area that allows them to make use of their creative problem solving skills to help people improve their lives.

- ☐ Community Affairs Coordinator
- ☐ Human Services Worker
- ☐ Family Law
- ☐ Political Activist
- ☐ Political Advisor
- ☐ Sign Language Interpreter
- ☐ Social Services Worker
- ☐ Social Worker

Technical

Authentic Blues are often able to bring a different perspective to technical positions. Because of their ability to build relationships they are able to bridge the gap between the technical and non-technical worlds. They make great liaisons between those developing the software and those with the subject matter expertise.[82] Furthermore, their ability to see the big picture and their creative problem solving skills often allow them to come up with unique solutions to technical problems.

- ☐ Computer Work: Explore all Categories
- ☐ Project Manager
- ☐ Engagement Manger
- ☐ Business Analyst
- ☐ Educational Software Developer
- ☐ Surveyor

Media and Public Relations

Authentic Blues often excel in communications. They have an ability to persuade others through their use of language. They make ideas and concepts easy to understand through their use of analogies and metaphors. Others tend to find them engaging and entertaining because of their story telling abilities. They are able to get to the heart of an issue because they connect with people and truly listen and understand. Authentic Blues often find positions in this field satisfying especially when they are dealing with issues they truly believe in.

- ❐ Advertising
- ❐ Copy Writer
- ❐ Editor Magazine, Book
- ❐ Fund-raiser
- ❐ Journalist, Reporter, Columnist
- ❐ Managing Editor
- ❐ Media/Public Relations Worker/Manager
- ❐ Motivational Speaker
- ❐ Multimedia Producer
- ❐ Radio or TV Producer
- ❐ Radio/ TV Broadcaster
- ❐ Public Relations Specialist
- ❐ Public Speaker
- ❐ Publicity Writer

Coaching, Counselling and Mediation

Authentic Blues have a strong belief in human potential and a need to help others grow and develop. This combined with their need for harmony, often drawn them to occupations in the coaching, counselling and mediation fields; these occupations allow them to connect with people. They take great pleasure in helping others, both individually and in groups, find fulfillment and happiness through self-understanding and awareness. They strive to help others communicate, find common ground, and resolve conflict. These occupations allow Authentic Blues to make use of their listening, awareness and communications skills. They can often get to the root of an issue by listening and observing. They can help people see both sides of an issue through exploration and communication. They often see possibilities and possible solutions that others may not. They then help people translate those into a reality for themselves. These occupations can be as fulfilling for the Authentic Blue as they are for the people they are helping.

- ❏ Career Development Practitioner
- ❏ Coach: Executive, Life Skills, Athletics
- ❏ Counsellor: Explore all categories
- ❏ Divorce Mediation
- ❏ Employment Development Specialist
- ❏ Family Mediation
- ❏ Facilitator
- ❏ Industrial/Labour Relations
- ❏ Labour Relations Mediator
- ❏ Mediator: Personnel or Personal
- ❏ Motivational Speaker
- ❏ Outplacement Counsellor/Coach
- ❏ Religion Oriented Occupations
- ❏ Team Building Consultant

Arts, Crafts and Entertainment

Authentic Blues are often drawn to the world of arts, crafts, and entertainment because it allows them to express themselves in creative and unique ways. It gives them the opportunity to communicate their own vision and ideas through many different mediums, such as through voice, written words, music, visual art, or theatre. They are continually able to develop in new and original ways. Often, what they create has a positive impact on others, which is important to Authentic Blues. As long as they can express themselves authentically they will be happy.

- ❏ Actor
- ❏ Architect
- ❏ Artist, Sculptor, Illustrator
- ❏ Composer, Lyricist

- ❏ Craft Worker
- ❏ Carpenter
- ❏ Designer
- ❏ Director: Movies, Radio, TV, Video
- ❏ Entertainer
- ❏ Fashion Designer or Illustrator
- ❏ Florist
- ❏ Graphic Design Artist
- ❏ Greeting Card Writer
- ❏ Interior Designer
- ❏ Jewellery Designer
- ❏ Musician
- ❏ Painter, Decorator
- ❏ Photographer
- ❏ Poet
- ❏ Publisher
- ❏ Set Designer
- ❏ Writer: Explore all categories

Authentic Blue Final Activity

What are the top ten careers that you would like to explore?

1.

2.

3.

4.

5.

6.

7.

8.

9.

10.

Both Canada and the United States have a number of web sites that you can use to explore careers in greater depth. Two that we would recommend are:

In Canada:
http://www.jobfutures.ca/en/home.shtml

In the USA:
www.jobbankinfo.org/

Section 6

The Abilities Associated with each Temperament

In chapter 1 we asked you to complete the Temperament questionnaire to help you get an idea of your preferred colour. We also mentioned earlier that Temperament theory states that our preferences are innate – we are born with a drive to act in a certain way based on our core needs and values. Linda Berens points out that our Temperament pattern has a high degree of influence over which skills we develop.[83] This is because we are more likely to develop skills in our preferred areas. Additionally, because we are all "plaid", we can and do to a greater or lesser degree develop skills and abilities that go with each of the Temperaments. However, as many of us are aware, we have a "least preferred" Temperament – one where our skills and abilities are less developed. This can sometimes hamper us as we are not always able to act flexibly enough to meet the needs of the moment. Because our abilities are not as well developed for that situation as they could be.

In chapters 12 through 15 we will examine some of the key abilities associated with each of the Temperaments. There are several abilities for each Temperament – we have mentioned only a few examples. This will give you the opportunity to examine the abilities associated with each Temperament so that you can determine which, if any, you need to develop to allow you to truly act flexibly in work situations. Through a series of exercises you will be able to practice the abilities that you would like to develop more fully.

12

Abilities Associated with Inquiring Greens

As we have seen earlier in the book Inquiring Greens have many abilities. Four of those are:

1. They have the ability to look at situations from a large-scale systems perspective, taking a macro rather than micro view of the world.

2. They are effective change agents, always looking for ways to improve the world in which they live by seeing possibilities and imagining things as they could be.

3. They can stay cool, calm, and collected – even in a crisis. The ability to control their emotions and present themselves in a calm way is a point of pride for Inquiring Greens.

4. They bring a healthy scepticism to everything that they are involved with. When they find a flaw in a system, idea, or process they have the ability to verbalize it logically to others.

Using Systems Thinking

What Inquiring Greens do so well is look at the world from a macro perspective. They see the whole forest, not the individual trees. This contrasts with the Organized Golds or the Resourceful Oranges who look at the world from a micro perspective. Inquiring Greens at their best are natural systems thinkers.

The Fifth Discipline Field Book defines a system as a "perceived whole" whose pieces connect because they affect each other over time and operate towards a common goal.[84] A system can be a biological system, such as how the body works, a political system such as how the politics of a country work, or an organizational system such as how a company actually functions. If we were looking at an organization from a systems perspective we would look at a broad range of interrelated facets, such as the hierarchy, processes, attitudes, perceptions, leadership, products, and services.

An effective systems thinker can see four different levels operating together at any one time: the events, patterns of behaviour, systems, and mental models.[85]

Events

When Inquiring Greens focus on events they describe the situation or problem as accurately as possible. It is important to stick to the known facts and evidence, by doing this avoid making assumptions about what is causing the problem or what the potential solution is. It is very tempting to create a biased problem statement that already suggests the solution, for example, "The problem is that our quality control process needs to be changed."

When describing events it is also important to avoid judging or blaming anyone. Assigning blame causes people to become defensive and resistant to looking at situations objectively.

Behavioural Patterns

When Inquiring Greens focus on patterns of behaviour, they work to identify long-term trends and determine their impact. The goal at this level is to look at the problem from as many different perspectives as possible so that they can unearth the habitual patterns of behaviour that have created the situation. Although this can sometimes be frustrating because some views may contradict others, it is in the analysis that Inquiring Greens will gain a greater understanding of the patterns underlying the situation.

It is important to consider the problem from many perspectives:

- How does management see the problem?
- How do other departments see the problem?

- How do the employees see the problem?
- How do your clients see the problem?

Structure of System

The next level of assessment works to uncover what caused the patterns of behaviour. This is the most powerful level to work at because Inquiring Greens we find the underlying causes of behaviour, then they can work to change the patterns of behaviour. It is useful to consider the following questions:

- Is the structure causing the problems?
- Are relationships contributing to the problems?
- Are people's assumptions a contributing factor?
- Are habitual patterns of behaviour contributing to the problem?
- Is the reward system at fault?
- Are the goals and values of an organization problematic?
- Is the leadership a problem?

Mental Models

Mental models are the perceptions, assumptions, visualizations, and stories that we have about ourselves, others, and the world in general. We form our mental models from our life experiences to date – our parents, schooling, upbringing, culture, and other life experiences. Mental models often act at an unconscious level to frame our thinking and behaviour. They are so powerful because they frame our perceptions of events. If you talk to two people who experienced the same event, such as a disruptive team meeting, you may get two very different descriptions of what happened based on their individual mental models. It is important to take the time to unearth our mental models, examine, and challenge them so that we do not make the same mistakes repeatedly.

Example

Let's apply these systems thinking concepts to a banking situation that we became involved in as consultants. A recurring problem at this particular bank was customer complaints that the customer service representatives (CSRs) were not providing effective customer service. In the past, the leaders had jumped to conclusions and assumed that the CSRs were not trained effectively. Their premature solution had been to give the CSRs yet another training course on customer service. This solution didn't resolve the problem. Finally, the leadership team decided to look at the events differently this time and search for any underlying behavioural patterns that existed.

They quickly identified a self-defeating pattern of behaviour they had used when trying to resolve the customer service problem. Each time they had been alerted to the customer service problem they assumed that training was the problem and implemented yet another training course. The only variation of the discussion was how to deliver the training; via classroom training, coaching, or the intranet. Interestingly enough, after a training session customer service did improve for a short period of time but then problems started to occur again. The leadership team realized that they needed to do some research to get the different perspectives from those involved before deciding how to resolve the issue. The research team conducted interviews with CSRs, managers, and supervisors and observed the CSRs in action.

Once the leadership team received the research results they began to see some of the underlying causes of the behaviour at the branch level. They found out that CSRs knew how to give good customer service because they received training on a number of occasions. When the CSRs completed a round of training customer service initially did improve. However, effective customer service was not rewarded; what was rewarded was processing as many people as possible especially when the lines were long. Administrative efficiency was the measure used not good customer service. At the end of the day management allowed those who completed all of their administrative tasks and balanced to leave early. Because they were not rewarded for providing good customer service the CSRs quickly returned to their usual behaviour. The leadership team began to realize that they needed to change the reward system within the branch.

The leadership team also decided to examine some of the mental models they used that might have contributed to the problem – especially those related to problem solving. Upon examination, they realized that when looking at problems they had developed habitual ways of looking at them. As a team, they did not take the time to explore all sides of a problem before jumping to conclusions. As a result they applied the same solution to a problem repeatedly, even when it did not work. This is not unusual in the problem solving process – because our favourite explanations "seem to work" most of the time, we often fail to question them, even when better ones are available. The leadership team decided that in the future, they would use a defined problem solving process that did not allow them to jump straight to conclusions. They also agreed that they would try to identify their mental models on an ongoing basis.

Application Activity

Now it is your turn to apply big picture thinking to a problem in your work environment. Choose a problem that has been around for a while where you know the history as this will enable you to think about underlying patterns. It is also best to choose a problem that is important but not so overwhelming that you will get lost in the complexity of it. Fill out the following chart to get a macro view of the problem.

1. The problem is:

2. What are the patterns of behaviour that have contributed to this issue over time?

3. What has caused these patterns of behaviour?

4. What mental models are at work in this situation?

Being a Change Agent

A **change agent**, or **agent of change**, is a person who intentionally or unintentionally causes or speeds up social, cultural, or behavioral change.[86] If we look a little deeper the first question we must ask ourselves is why does a change agent do what they do – what is it inside them that makes them want to cause or accelerate social, cultural, or behavioural change? Change agents live in the future; they are not bound to the past or the present. They have a vision of what they think could or should be and use it as their motivation to make change happen. They are not satisfied with the status quo and they have a vision of how much better the future could be.

From earlier discussions about Inquiring Greens we can see that they fit the definition of a change agent. When they are at their best they are always looking for ways to improve the world in which they live. They are quite often visionary thinkers and have the ability to see possibilities and imagine the world as it could be.

As we discussed earlier in this chapter taking a systems thinking approach is the way many Inquiring Greens handle life. This approach can be very useful when it comes to being a change agent. They start with the big picture of the overall change. Then they use a very logical and knowledge-based approach to ask some tough, insightful questions like:

- Why are we making the change?
- Will this change cause positive long term improvements?
- What effect will this change have on our bottom line?
- Is our approach the best one to take or could we approach this differently?
- Do we have the expertise and resources necessary to carry this out effectively?

As we can see by these questions, Inquiring Greens are often able to add value to the change process by looking at it with a critical eye, seeing potential flaws, and coming up with ways to refine and improve it.

A broad, long term results oriented approach to change helps the Inquiring Green avoid jumping in too fast and making quick fixes. In the long run, quick fixes usually only fix the symptoms and not the root cause of the problem. This results in a lack of real long term improvements. Because Inquiring Greens take a broad approach they tend to look at the organization as a whole. They help ensure that changes will be aligned with the overall organizational goals and vision and will often refine the objectives and goals of a change until they are sure it is in keeping with the vision and goals of the organization and that it will move the organization towards long term improvements. As they prefer to focus on broad changes that have a global impact, Inquiring Greens are not always interested in the implementation details of a change. However, they do like to see changes come to fruition in a timely manner so they will be a driving force in ensuring they are implemented successfully.[87]

Application Activity

Think of a change you would like to have happen. It can be either professional or personally oriented.

Ask yourself the following questions:

1. Why am I/we making the change?

2. Will this change cause positive long term improvements?

3. What effect will this change have on my or my organization's bottom line?

4. Is my/our approach the best one to take or could I approach this differently?

5. Do I/we have the expertise and resources necessary to carry this out effectively?

6. Do I still want to make this change?

Being Cool, Calm and Collected

At their best, Inquiring Greens prefer to stay cool, calm and collected – even in a crisis. They are able to control their emotions, both internally and externally. To do this internally they:

- **Take time to think before reacting**. First, they give themselves the time to think through a situation before making a decision. Then, they consider potential consequences before acting.

- **Come from a place of logic rather than emotion when making a decision**. By making use of their intelligence and knowledge they are able to logically think through a situation. They weigh the pros and cons, determine what the potential consequences will be, and analyze whether the decision will have a positive out come.

- **Don't let their urges take over**. They make use of their intelligence and knowledge to overpower emotional urges. In addition, if emotions do come into play they are able to calm down quickly by going to a place of logic.

Inquiring Greens work hard to present a calm exterior. If they feel worried or excited it probably won't show. They demonstrate this through their body language and tone of voice, which are key ways others interpret us. In his widely quoted article, Albert Mehrabian, stated that the words we use actually account for less than 10% of the message we convey. The balance is communicated through our body language and tone of voice.[88]

There are a number of aspects to body language, facial expression, postures and gestures, and spatial relationships. Many Inquiring

Greens are adept at making use of all of them to demonstrate a calm exterior.

The face is the most expressive part of the body. Positive emotions, such as happiness, love, and surprise are the easiest to recognize. Although negative emotions such as sadness, anger, and disgust are also conveyed through facial expression. The Inquiring Green is often good at masking their facial expression. The term "poker face" describes an attempt to keep others from knowing your true feelings. The eyes are an excellent indicator of a person's feelings. Generally, during a conversation both the listener and the speaker will tend to "look" and then "look away". They will look at one another from one to ten seconds before looking away again. Usually, we look at a person when discussing a pleasant topic, for example, what we are going to do on our holidays. Conversely, if we are discussing an unpleasant or embarrassing topic, such as a mistake made by one or other of the people in the discussion, we are more likely to avoid eye contact. Inquiring Greens are often very good at making sure they do not give anything away through their eye contact.

People also reveal their attitudes and feelings by the way they stand or sit and the way they move their body. We take it as a compliment when someone leans towards us in a conversation, probably because their posture suggests that they are interested and involved in the conversation. However, a slumped posture can be a sign of feeling depressed or tired. Many Inquiring Greens pay attention to their posture making sure they lean towards someone when they are involved in a conversation. In addition, they do not slump or slouch.

Positioning of arms and legs can also communicate how a person is thinking or feeling. For example, crossed arms can signal defensiveness. Conversely, open arms extended towards you generally indicate openness and acceptance. Again, Inquiring Greens are aware of the positioning of their arms and legs and the message it may be sending.

How closely we space ourselves in relation to each other is another important factor in communication. North American studies have shown that the distance between people when in conversation depends largely on the type of interaction. For example, friends usually place themselves closer together, while business associates tend to keep a distance of approximately 3 ft. Generally, Inquiring Greens will make a point to stand or sit within the appropriate distance for a given type of transaction.

Next to body language, tone of voice can give the most useful clues about a person's message. The volume and pitch are helpful to the listener when trying to decode a person's message. Enthusiasm, joy, anger, and fear tend to be expressed in a higher pitch, as well as in a wider range of tone and volume. Emotions like sadness, despair, and grief are usually spoken softly and in a lower pitch. Many Inquiring Greens are quite adept at keeping their vocal expression very neutral and calm.

A person's rate of speech also conveys their feelings. Most people tend to speed up their speech rate when they are excited or anxious. On the other hand, people tend to talk more slowly when depressed or tired. Inquiring Greens are often able to keep a nice, even rate of speech, thereby not allowing others to know what their true feelings are.

Presenting yourself as calm, cool, and collected can be very useful because:
- You tend to be less stressed because you are not emotionally invested in everything that you do.
- You use your energy to accomplish things rather than react to them.
- People trust and respect you because you are not likely to loose your cool.
- People are more candid with you because they don't fear how you will respond.
- People take your emotions seriously when you do display them at a crucial time.

Application Activity

Think of a difficult situation that you need to deal with in the future in which you need to be cool, calm, and collected.

1. How will you control you emotions internally?

2. What will you do to present a calm exterior?

Being Sceptical and Critiquing

Inquiring Greens bring a healthy scepticism to everything in which they are involved. They are often able to logically analyze the situation and find the flaw in an idea, a plan, or a project. They do this by making use of systems thinking abilities discussed earlier in this chapter. When listening to an idea or looking at a plan or project they will ask themselves questions such as:

- Is it logical?
- Why are we doing this?
- Is there a different approach that we could take?
- Will it improve the long term situation?
- Do we have the ability and resources to do this?
- Is there a flaw and, if so, what is the flaw?

Inquiring Greens are not scared to voice their opinions and fight for what they believe is right. They will do this in a very logical manner and don't believe in bringing emotion of any kind into a reasoned argument. When they express their opinions effectively, they do it in an assertive not aggressive manner.

Robert Bolton indicates that a useful way to define assertion is to place it in a continuum between submissive and aggressive behaviour and to look at the differences between each type of behaviour.[89]

Submissive Behaviour	Assertive Behaviour	Aggressive Behaviour

Submissive Behaviour

When people use submissive behaviour they show a lack of respect for their own needs and rights. Some submissive people do not express their honest feelings, needs, values, and concerns. They find it hard to state what they want or need when, generally, that's all it would take to have their needs met. When they do express their needs they do it in such an apologetic and meek way that others do not take them seriously.

When people are being submissive, they demonstrate this approach through their body language. They tend to use inoffensive words and their voice tone tends to be soft. Their eyes may be downcast and they frequently give limited or no eye contact. Often they try to make themselves look smaller than they actually are. They may have excessive head nodding and their hands can be fidgety or fluttery.

Assertive Behaviour

The assertive person presents himself or herself in a way that maintains self-respect and works towards the satisfaction of needs without dominating or abusing others. Assertive people stand up for their own rights and express themselves in straightforward and appropriate ways. However, the stance is win-win because they do not want to violate the needs of others.

Assertive people's body language reflects their assertive stance. They generally have an assured manner with an erect but relaxed posture. Voice tone is usually firm and loud enough for everyone to hear. They tend to face other people squarely and their body movements are relaxed and open. Assertive people maintain eye contact with others but not in a fixed or staring way.

Aggressive Behaviour

A person using aggressive behaviour communicates feelings, needs, and wants at the expense of others. This person's goal is always to win arguments. Their voice tone is generally loud and they can be abusive, rude, or domineering. Their point of view is most important and what others want is of lesser importance.

A person using aggressive behaviour tends to have a stiff or rigid posture and may use a range of domineering gestures such as hands on hips, clenched hands, pointing finger, or pounding on a desk. Their voice may be tense, shrill, loud, or demanding. Frequently their eyes bore into the other person. They want to make themselves seem larger than they actually are.

As you can see from the definitions above it is important to place yourself on the center of the continuum and behave in an assertive manner when expressing your opinions.

Application Activity

When you are in a meeting where plans, ideas, and projects are being presented put on your critiquing hat. Ask yourself:

1. Are the plans, ideas, projects, etc. being put forward logical?

2. Is there a flaw?

3. Is the timing right to critique the ideas?

4. How will I present my critique in an assertive way?

13

Abilities Associated with Resourceful Oranges

As we have seen earlier in the book Resourceful Oranges have many abilities. Four of these abilities are:

1. The ability to persuade others in a non-coercive and non-manipulative way.

2. The ability to be a skilled risk-taker, taking calculated risks based on a good understanding of a situation.

3. The ability to be adaptable and deal with a crisis.

4. The ability to be optimistic.

Persuading Others

When we persuade others we use a variety of different techniques to influence them. Effective persuasion does not use coercive techniques, nor is it manipulative. Rather, we encourage people to adopt an idea, an approach, or an action by using techniques that get them to buy in to our approach. This is a crucial skill in the flatter, leaner, less hierarchical workplace of today where we need to influence our peers, our team, our manager, and other key stakeholders.

Activity: Persuasion Quiz

Before we discuss a couple of persuasive techniques in detail, please ask someone you know who will be honest with you to complete the following persuasion quiz about you.

Persuasion Quiz	YES	NO
1. Does he or she tailor his or her arguments to the person that they are trying to influence?		
2. Does he or she put him or herself in the other person's shoes and understand what they want?		
3. Does he or she present him or herself in a credible manner?		
4. Does he or she listen to the person they are trying to influence?		
5. Does he or she use a positive approach?		
6. Does he or she present his or her viewpoint clearly?		
7. Does he or she use a variety of techniques to persuade the listener?		

The more "yes" answers, the more persuasive you are likely to be. Let's review why the "yes" answers indicate persuasiveness.

1. Tailor your arguments to the person that you are trying to influence

Think about the person that you are trying to influence. How much do they know about the topic? How do they like to receive information? What are their goals, needs, and concerns in this situation? Do they like details or the big picture? Once you answer some of these questions you will be able to determine your most effective approach.

2. Put yourself in the other person's shoes and understand what they want

Think about what the other person wants, what arguments will persuade them, and how they will benefit.

3. Present yourself in a credible manner

Do your homework – make sure that you know your facts and are prepared to respond knowledgeably to questions and concerns. If you do have established credentials or qualifications in a given area it can be helpful to make these known to the other person.

4. Listen to the person you are trying to influence

Listen to what the other person has to say about your arguments. If you understand their perspective you will be able to respond appropriately to their comments and concerns. Also, observe their body language. Often a person's body language communicates what they are truly thinking or feeling.

5. Use a positive approach

First, assume that the person you are speaking to is an intelligent, reasonable person. Take a win-win approach and never talk down to them. Demonstrate respect by your words and actions.

6. Present your viewpoint clearly

Determine your goal in the communication process. Identify three to five key points that will persuade the listener. Think about how you will present these points clearly.

7. Use a variety of techniques to persuade your listener

Whenever possible develop a variety of techniques to persuade your listener. Make sure that you can present your points in a logical, rational manner. At the same time think about how you can approach a person on an emotional level. Also, present your argument in an interesting and engaging manner. Where possible inject fun and get the other person involved by asking questions.

We will now focus on a couple of techniques that will help you to become more persuasive. The first technique looks at how to analyze your audience. The second technique focuses on how to present your views in a persuasive manner.

Analyze your Audience

Earlier we discussed the importance of putting yourself in the other person's shoes to determine what they want. Once you understand what they want, you can use this information to persuade them that your suggestions will meet their own needs. In other words, people need to know "What's in it for me?" if you are going to obtain their cooperation.

When identifying the needs of others, you might want to consider the following:

1. Goals and objectives

2. Needs and values

3. Motivation

4. Working relationships with others

5. The work they do: roles and responsibilities

6. Power, status, identity

Activity: Analyze the People You want to Persuade

1. Think of a situation where you need to persuade another person or a group of people. Briefly describe the situation.

2. Identify the person or people that you need to persuade. For each, analyze his or her needs.

Person	What are his/her needs in this situation?

Develop a Persuasive Argument or Approach

How can you present your ideas and recommendations in a persuasive way? Gary Hankins in his book *The Power of the Pitch* suggests how to structure and package your message for maximum effect by using the Issue – Solution – Benefits (ISB) model.[90] The model has three parts to it; the first part identifies the issue under discussion, the second part focuses on the solution and last part outlines the benefits of the solution. This model can be used to persuade another person or group in a face-to-face discussion or in writing. It can also be used to make a presentation to a team or large group.

Issue

Begin by discussing the problems, issues, or challenges in the situation and outline why they are causing concern for the person or group you wish to persuade. It is important to look at the situation from the other person's perspective and identify why the current situation is problematic for them, not for you. Once you have discussed the issue and identified why it is problematic, it is often useful to ask for confirmation that others see the issue the same way that you do. They will confirm either that they agree with you or give you additional information regarding how they see the issue.

As Gary Hankins points out, most concerns center around time (not enough time), money (making money, too little, protecting what they have), success (how to be successful) people (not enough, not sufficiently trained), space (not enough, or not the right space), or quality (need for improvement).

The rationale behind starting with their issues first is that if you want to persuade someone you must first focus on what their challenges are before you show that you have a way to resolve them.

Solution

The next step in the process is to discuss the solution to the issues that you have just identified. Discuss how your proposed solution will help resolve the problem that they are experiencing. Be detailed enough that they understand what your solution is without bogging them down in unnecessary details and confusing them.

Benefits

Focus on the benefits that the individual, team, or group will receive by adopting the solution that you have outlined. Emphasizing benefits is important because people always want to know how they, the team, or the organization will benefit from the proposed solution.

Remember that when using this approach there should always be a give and take discussion at each stage. The more that you can understand the other person's perspective and respond to their concerns, the easier they will be to persuade.

Activity: Develop a Persuasive Argument or Approach

Earlier, we asked you to think of a situation where you need to persuade another person or a group of people. We also asked you to briefly describe that situation and identify the needs of the people involved.

Now work through the ISB model to determine how you would persuade them.

The ISB Approach	
What are the problems, concerns, or challenges in this situation for the other party?	
What solution would you recommend?	
What are the benefits of that solution to the other party/ parties?	

Being a Skilled Risk Taker

Being a skilled risk taker doesn't mean that you are reckless or take a risk just for the sake of taking one. It is more about being able to enter into a new or unfamiliar situation without feeling anxious. It is also about having the self-confidence to investigate new things, find out what they are all about, and weigh the pros and cons before proceeding. Once the skilled risk taker decides to move ahead they are able to defend their decision in a rational manner because they really believe in what they are doing. The skilled risk taker is one who takes calculated risks based on a good understanding of a situation and the knowledge that they have more to gain than loose by continuing.

The Importance of Being a Risk Taker

In this day and age, when individuals and organizations seem to spend so much time trying to avoid or mitigate risks, we may ask ourselves why is it important to be a risk taker? Without risk there would be no creativity or innovation. Individuals and organizations willing to take risks will gain the competitive edge and be successful. If Richard Branson had not been willing to take the necessary risks to turn his vision into reality he would not have been able to create one of the most recognizable brands in the world. As we mentioned in chapter 3, he managed to "Virginize" a very wide number of products and services ranging from airlines, credit cards, books, to trains. Even today, he is always looking for new challenges such as entering markets dominated by a few key players. He truly is a skilled risk taker.

To move successfully ahead in an organization you must be willing to take some calculated risks. David Cumberbatch, a director at a business psychology firm, Xancam, advises us to concentrate on doing activities that will have the greatest return, not just the ones that are safe.[91]

This approach may attract some criticism along the way. However, when it does work out you will get noticed and praised. In today's job market, that is a necessary part of moving ahead in an organization. The key is knowing when and how to take calculated risks.

How to Become a Skilled Risk Taker

Here are 5 steps to help you become a more skilled risk taker, adapted from a list by James J Messina in his article "*Becoming a Risk Taker.*"[92]

1. Determine your willingness to take risks.

2. Be willing to move outside your comfort zone.

3. Seek out activities and situations that will likely deliver the best return.

4. Measure the risks of failure against the rewards of success.

5. Concentrate on positive outcomes.

Step 1 – Determine your willingness to take risks

The first step in becoming a skilled risk taker is to determine your own willingness to take risks. There are many quizzes and assessments available to help you determine this. Answering the following set of questions can help to give you a sense:

Circle the letter that best describes you.

1. I totally agree with the statement "there is no greater risk than taking no risk at all".

   a. This statement is very true of me

   b. This statement is somewhat true of me

   c. This statement is neither true nor false about me

   d. This statement is somewhat false about me

   e. This statement is very false about me

2. I am willing to try new things even if they go against convention.

   a. This statement is very true of me

   b. This statement is somewhat true of me

   c. This statement is neither true nor false about me

   d. This statement is somewhat false about me

   e. This statement is very false about me

3. By taking risks I am able to experience new things and learn new skills.

   a. This statement is very true of me

   b. This statement is somewhat true of me

   c. This statement is neither true nor false about me

   d. This statement is somewhat false about me

   e. This statement is very false about me

4. I like to do things even if the outcome is unknown.

    a. This statement is very true of me

    b. This statement is somewhat true of me

    c. This statement is neither true nor false about me

    d. This statement is somewhat false about me

    e. This statement is very false about me

5. When taking a calculated risk I feel confident in what I am doing.

    a. This statement is very true of me

    b. This statement is somewhat true of me

    c. This statement is neither true nor false about me

    d. This statement is somewhat false about me

    e. This statement is very false about me

6. I enjoy playing dangerous sports even if I know I can get seriously hurt by doing so.

    a. This statement is very true of me

    b. This statement is somewhat true of me

    c. This statement is neither true nor false about me

    d. This statement is somewhat false about me

    e. This statement is very false about me

7. I never feel playing it safe is the best policy.

    a. This statement is very true of me

    b. This statement is somewhat true of me

    c. This statement is neither true nor false about me

    d. This statement is somewhat false about me

    e. This statement is very false about me

8. I consider risk taking to be a great way to experience new things.

   a. This statement is very true of me

   b. This statement is somewhat true of me

   c. This statement is neither true nor false about me

   d. This statement is somewhat false about me

   e. This statement is very false about me

9. I consider myself to be decisive and am willing to take risks.

   a. This statement is very true of me

   b. This statement is somewhat true of me

   c. This statement is neither true nor false about me

   d. This statement is somewhat false about me

   e. This statement is very false about me

10. If I had the opportunity to move to a new country to take a job that paid double or triple what I currently earn I would jump at it.

   a. This statement is very true of me

   b. This statement is somewhat true of me

   c. This statement is neither true nor false about me

   d. This statement is somewhat false about me

   e. This statement is very false about me

SCORING:

If you circled mainly:

   a - You are very willing to take risks; perhaps at times a little too willing to do so.

   b - You are willing to take risks; however, you tend to think twice before doing so which is good.

c - You are neither willing to take risks or risk adverse.

d - You are somewhat risk adverse.

e - You are very risk adverse.

Step 2 – Be willing to move outside your comfort zone

If you tend to be risk adverse or even neutral about your willingness to take risks you will need to push yourself further than you normally do by putting yourself in situations that may feel uncomfortable. The more that you do this the easier it will become.

Step 3 – Seek out activities and situations that will likely deliver the best return

For the third step, look for risks that are really worth taking or that will potentially deliver the best return. Don't always play it safe, by playing it safe you are not likely to get hurt however, you are not likely to gain much either.

Step 4 – Measure the risks of failure against the rewards of success

Take a hard look at the activity or situation you have chosen and make a list of the rewards you will gain by taking the risk. Make a second list indicating why you might potentially fail. If the rewards that you will gain from success outweigh the potential for failure, then go for it. You won't always succeed, but in the long run you will come out ahead.

Step 5 – Concentrate on positive outcomes

Look at the list of reasons why you might fail and think about ways you can mitigate or eliminate them. As much as possible set yourself up for success. As you move forward, keep in mind the list of rewards you will gain from a positive outcome. If you truly believe you can achieve a positive outcome then the likelihood of success is much greater.

Becoming a Skilled Risk Taker Activity

If you completed an assessment of your willingness to take risks and found that you are at least somewhat risk adverse, then the next step is to identify an activity or situation that will take you outside your comfort zone.

In the space below write an activity or situation that will take you outside your comfort zone.

Next, make a list of rewards you are likely to gain from this activity or situation. Then, make a list of potential reasons why you might fail. Compare the lists. If the rewards seem to outweigh the risks of failure then continue.

Rewards	Potential Reasons for Failure

Then look at your list of reasons why you might fail and think about ways you can mitigate or eliminate those reasons.

Finally, while you are involved in the activity or situation keep in mind the list of rewards you will gain from a positive outcome. Remember, if you truly believe you can achieve a positive outcome then the likelihood of a positive outcome is greatly increased.

Being Adaptable and Dealing with Crisis Situations

Many Resourceful Oranges have the ability to adapt quickly to changing situations. They are able to think on their feet, react rapidly, and keep calm in stressful situations. As a result, they are able to respond expediently to crises situations. This is an important ability to possess in today's shifting work environment where organizations need to react quickly to unforeseen factors such as economic disasters, health epidemics, or terrorist attacks.

Adaptability and Flexibility

As stated in the book *Emotional Intelligence in Action: Training and Coaching Activities for Leaders and Managers*, flexible people are like willow trees in that they can bend a long way in a stormy situation that would damage thicker trees.[93] They have the ability to shift quickly when something unexpected occurs. When given new information, or when a change occurs, they are able to assess the situation and act accordingly. They don't get bogged down by how things should be or by sticking to the pre-arranged plan. This contrasts with less adaptable people who have a tendency to become scared or rigid when faced with change.

There are many advantages to becoming more adaptable in business and personal life:

- Change is a constant in every part of our life and our success will depend on our ability to adapt.

- When we adapt to changing circumstances we are generally happier because we are no longer fearful.

- Adapting also enables us to remain physically and emotionally healthier because resistance saps our resources.

Three abilities that will help you increase your adaptability and flexibility are:

1. Looking at the benefits inherent in any new challenge

Rather than thinking to themselves "this change is going to be for the worst"; adaptable people ask themselves "how can I benefit by this change?" They answer the question "what is in it for me?"

Additionally, they use their creativity to explore options when adapting to a change. They brainstorm a list of alternatives and then review them to determine what the most expedient way of handling the change is.

Activity: Benefits and Options

Think of an upcoming change that you need to adapt to in your life.

1. How can you benefit from this change?

2. What are your options in adapting to this change?

2. Identifying your negative beliefs about yourself

We are all able to adapt and change. However, some of us stop ourselves from adapting as easily as we could because of our negative beliefs about ourselves. We receive these messages as we grow up from our cultural environment, including the influences of our, school, and society. As we grow older, we internalize these messages and make them into our own beliefs. Typical negative messages that we give ourselves are "I'm not intelligent, I will fail, no one will like me, I will never get the job I want, etc." These beliefs cause us to become afraid and we then tend to act in a rigid, unbending manner. We convince ourselves that we will fail if we try anything new or that others will make fun of us.

It is important that we surface our negative beliefs about ourselves so that we no longer act from a deep-seated psychological stance. Once we identify them we can examine them, refute them, and replace them with positive beliefs.

Activity: Identify your Negative Beliefs About Yourself

Identify three negative beliefs that you have about yourself:

1.

2.

3.

Now review your list of negative beliefs. Ask yourself how you can replace them with empowering beliefs. For example, if you said, "I can't do this," an empowering belief would be "I can learn to do this." Through positive beliefs you will learn to feel more powerful.

1.

2.

3.

3. Being Resilient

Resilient people adapt effectively when they face change, challenges, and stress. They have a series of coping strategies that enable them to get back on their feet and carry on.[94]

There are a number of strategies you can use to build your resilience:

- Develop an effective support system. We all maintain a variety of relationships with family, friends, and co-workers. People who draw strength from these relationships are able to deal with problems that they would not be able to deal with on their own. In sharing our problems with significant others in our lives we tend to gain the energy and strength to manage them. Don't be scared to reach out to your support system and ask for help when you need it.

- Have fun and don't forget to play. Having fun and playing are critical to becoming re-energized because they help release built up tension, connect us to others, and help us to think creatively.

- Resist seeing crises as insurmountable problems. Life happens and along with it we will encounter our fair share of stressful experiences. Try looking beyond the present to how circumstances in the future may improve. Notice and acknowledge when things improve even slightly.

- Set realistic goals and always take steps to move towards them. Don't wait until you have a large block of time to move towards your goals. Constantly ask yourself what small steps you can take to move forward.

- Treat everything as a learning opportunity. We can learn from both the positive and negative experiences in our life. Sometimes we learn most from the challenges that present themselves to us.

- Be kind to yourself. Focus on what you do well and acknowledge your strengths. Do not focus on your weaknesses. As discussed earlier, see them as learning opportunities.

Dealing with crisis situations

Resourceful Oranges tend to thrive in crisis because they have the ability to think on their feet and be practical problem solvers. They are often attracted to careers such as fire fighting and emergency management services where these abilities are highly prized. They also do well in business environments where "fire fighting" is an asset. Let's review the abilities that enable people to handle emergencies of all types effectively. We will use the acronym **CPR** to discuss some of the key skills.

Calm. People who effectively handle emergencies remain calm. They do not panic and nor do they cause others to panic. They communicate by their words, body language, and tone of voice that they are in control of themselves and able to think rationally. If you find it difficult to remain calm in emergency situations and tend to panic, remember to take some deep breaths. Under stress we may have a tendency to breathe shallowly and therefore deprive ourselves of sufficient oxygen to think clearly. So take deep calming breaths until you feel under control and can think about you best strategy.

Prioritize. There are three steps involved in prioritizing:

1. Quickly asses the situation to determine what is currently happening. This may involve gathering information from others. You may also need to assess the readiness of others to determine whom you can enlist to help deal with the situation.

2. Think of the possible actions you can take to deal with the situation. When thinking of possible actions it is often useful to think in terms of those issues that you have control over versus those issues that you cannot control. Focus on those issues that you have immediate control over. Those challenges that you have no control over can be dealt with later or by calling in expert resources, e.g. an emergency response team.

3. For the possible actions that you can take, prioritize by determining what is most important and urgent. Start with these actions.

Respond. Once you have determined the best place to start – act. Do not waste time worrying about circumstances that you cannot control or things that you cannot change. Act in the moment to do your best with the situation. If possible, mobilize other people to help. Most people would prefer to be doing something to handle a crisis rather than passively watching what is happening.

Activity: How to Deal with a Crisis

1. Think of a crisis that you have handled in the past. Using the acronym **CPR** identify what you did well.

2. Now identify what you would like to do differently when you have to handle a crisis in the future.

Being Optimistic

An optimist is someone who tends to look at things from a positive perspective and generally believes that some good can be found in any situation. The old saying the glass is half full not half empty truly sums up an optimistic view of life.

There are many advantages to being an optimist. Optimistic people tend to be productive in all areas of their lives. At work, they are able to keep better focused and achieve more because they don't get bogged down in negativity and feelings of doubt. Others enjoy working with them because of their positive and supportive approach. Therefore they are much less likely to be involved in conflict with a co-worker. Optimists tend to see problems as opportunities that can lead to more innovative solutions. Overall, optimistic people tend to feel enthusiastic about their work, which leads to a much more productive, and enjoyable work environment for everyone involved.[95]

How to have an optimist viewpoint

Even if you have always had a pessimistic viewpoint, it is possible to turn things around and become more optimistic. Here are a few simple steps that can help you become more optimistic.

1. **Determine how much of an optimist or pessimist you really are**

   First, figure out just how optimistic or pessimistic you really are. There are several quizzes and assessments available on the internet, all you need to do is enter "optimism test" into any search engine and a list of different ones will come up. Once you know where you fall on the optimism/pessimism scale then you can decide how much work you will need to do to become more of an optimist.

2. **Figure out the root cause of your pessimism**

   The next step is to figure out where your pessimism really comes from. The root causes of pessimism are very similar to the root causes of negative self-beliefs discussed earlier in this chapter. Often deep-rooted negativity can be traced back to our childhood experiences.

3. **Rethink your assumptions towards your life**

   As we discussed about our negative beliefs, you need to rethink your assumptions. If you have persuaded yourself that the world is out to get you or that you live under a dark cloud you need to learn to let it go. It is both self-centred and irrational to believe that the universe has chosen you out of everyone else to make your existence miserable. While it is true that bad things sometimes happen, they happen to all of us. However, if you always assume the worst you can end up creating a negative self-fulfilling prophecy because you talk yourself into not allowing any good to come into your life.

4. **Don't dwell in the past**

   Just because something negative has happened to you in the past it does not mean that everything you do in the future will have a bad outcome. The key is to learn from what happened in the past, figure out what if any thing you could have done differently and move on. Don't let pessimism turn you into someone who avoids risks at all costs. As we discussed earlier in this chapter being a skilled risk taker is a good thing and sometimes it is necessary to take calculated risks to receive rewards. Just because a day or a week starts off badly it does not mean that it has to continue that way. Think about what you can do differently and concentrate on the good that is or could be happening.

5. **Control your life, don't let it control you**

   Don't become a victim of your circumstances. Stop looking at life as happening to you and think about what you can do to control how it happens. If your life is not going the way you want it to, rethink how you would like it to be, set some goals and move towards them.

6. **Embrace the good and release the bad**

   To be able to do this you need to accept that disappointment, failure, or pain is a part of life. However, they are not all that life has to offer. As we talked about earlier, life involves risk and not every risk has a good outcome – that is what makes it a risk. Yet, if we don't take those calculated risks then we are never going to experience the positives that come from taking them. Because life is a mix of good and bad it is important to embrace the good when it happens. Experience it to its fullest and enjoy it. The more you do that the more your expectations will improve and the less upsetting the bad will seem when it does happen. To help you identify the good write a list of the positive things that have happened to you in your life. Depending on your level of pessimism it may take you a while to make the list – but stick with it. The key to having an optimistic outlook is to see the possibilities in any situation and to recognize that life could always be worse. If you are having trouble making your list think about something in your life and how it could be worse and then flip that around and you will start to see the positive. For example, "I just have been downsized" could be flipped around to "now I have the opportunity to start my own business and my severance will give me the money to live on while I get it established." Once you have completed your list tuck it in an easily accessible place and when you are feeling down pull it out and read it to remind yourself that life is not all bad.

7. Make use of positive affirmations

Earlier in this chapter we talked about the importance of positive beliefs or affirmations. You can use this concept to put into words what you are trying to change about your view of the world. To do this you will want to write down short positive statements that will become reminders to you. You will then place these notes where you are likely to see them every day. Places like your bathroom mirror, the inside of your locker, the edge of your computer monitor, or even the dashboard of your car are appropriate. Some affirmations you may want to think about using are:

    a. I can do anything I put my mind to

    b. I make my own decisions, therefore I always have a choice

    c. I control my life, it does not control me

8. Remember that life is too short to waste on pessimistic thoughts

If you have the dark cloud of pessimism hanging over you remind yourself that life is short and you want to make every minute count. The more time you spend focused on the negatives the less time you will have available to focus on the positives in life. If you think about it, being pessimistic is a waste of time because you spend excessive amounts of time dwelling on things that haven't happened yet and probably never will happen. As a result the time you spend being pessimistic prevents you from spending your time productively to achieve your goals. Pessimism is a waste of time, and as time is such a limited resource you really can't afford to take it for granted.

9. Always keep balance in your life

Finally, always keep balance in your life. We are not suggesting that you pretend nothing bad is ever going to happen. That is not realistic and doing so could lead to poor decision making and allow others to take advantage of you. Having a healthy amount of pessimism in your life is actually an effective skill. It allows you to prepare for the worst but at the same time hope for the best. In doing so you are being sensible while at the same time keeping your life open to all of the possibilities it has to offer.

Application Activity

1. Determine how much of an optimist or pessimist you really are.

   Complete an online Optimism Assessment; type "optimism test" into your favourite search engine and a list of different ones will come up. If you find your level of Optimism is low, work your way through the following 8 Steps:

2. Figure out the root cause of your pessimism

3. Rethink your assumptions towards your life

4. Don't dwell in the past

5. Control your life, don't let it control you

6. Embrace the good and release the bad

7. Make use of positive affirmations

8. Remember that life is too short to waste on pessimistic thoughts

9. Always keep balance in your life

14

Abilities Associated with Organized Golds

As we have seen earlier in the book Organized Golds have many abilities. Four of these abilities are:

1. Managing their own time by being goal oriented and completing tasks in a timely manner combined with their strong work ethic.

2. Organizing and planning, whether it is for themselves, a project, a department, or a team.

3. Holding themselves and others to very high standards by being willing to correct and improve their own and other's work. They are detailed, able to find and correct mistakes, and give constructive feedback.

4. Maintaining corporate culture through their social consciousness. They are the caretakers of values, customs, traditions, and meanings and maintain the status quo within the organization.

We will now look at these four skill sets in greater detail.

Having Effective Time Management Skills

Organized Golds generally possess effective time management skills because they value being efficient and productive. Over the years, they have developed a set of abilities that enable them to manage their time effectively and accomplish tasks within the required time frames. We will focus on four key time management skills: understanding your strengths and weaknesses in managing your time, setting goals, identifying priorities, and using a "To Do" list.

Understanding time management strengths and challenges

The first step in managing your time more effectively is to identify both your time management strengths and challenges. Then you can focus on making changes in those areas that most need improvement.

Strengths and Challenges Activity

This quick survey will help determine your time management strengths and challenges at work. Read each of the following items and put a check mark under the appropriate letter that describes how effectively you handle each item. Use the following rating scheme:

E – for excellent

S – for satisfactory

N – for needs improvement

TIME MANAGEMENT AREA	YOUR RATING		
	E	S	N
Set and achieve objectives			
Plan and organize your work			
Prioritize tasks			
Handle paperwork			
Manage telephone interruptions			
Manage people interruptions			
Deal with crisis situations			
Manage your telephone time			
Let go of papers and possessions			
Follow-up appropriately			

Handle your reading load			
Manage your filing system			
Manage technology			
Manage e-mails			
Manage your calendar			
Make habit changes in how you do things			
Attend to quality issues and/or customer service			
Optimize the layout and location of your work space			
Handle flexible time such as work from home days			
Handle meetings (which to attend, length, etc.)			
Maintain a tidy, organized desk			
Overcome procrastination			
Say "No" when appropriate			
Make the most of travel time			
Handle work communications			
Deal with teamwork			
Manage work/life balance			
Deal with perfectionist tendencies			
Other			

Now on what areas should you concentrate?

Look at the Ns you have checked. Decide which three Ns are most in need of improvement. Take a few minutes to jot these key areas in the space provided below. For each of the key areas, identify what you could do to manage your time more effectively in these areas.

Three areas most in need of improvement are:

Area #1:

How can I manage my time more effectively in this area?

Area #2:

How can I manage my time more effectively in this area?

Area #3:

How can I manage my time more effectively in this area?

Setting goals and objectives

Effective time managers set goals on a daily, weekly, monthly, and yearly basis. All the time management tools and techniques in the world won't be of any use to you if you don't know where you are headed, that is, what you want to accomplish.

When developing goals and objectives keep the **SMART** acronym in mind, and make sure that your goals are.[96]

Specific – Make sure that you clarify exactly what you need to achieve. Your goals should be as specific as possible because then you will know precisely what you need to achieve. Express objectives in simple direct terms. Use action words such as organize, write, coordinate, lead, develop, plan, build, etc. Break down complex goals into smaller understandable objectives.

Measurable – How will you know when you reach your goal? Develop objectives that you can measure "Each day I will tackle my email inbox so that there are zero emails when I leave at the end of the day."

Achievable – Objectives need to be achievable so that you keep motivated and work towards their accomplishment. On the other hand, objectives still need to stretch you, but not so far that you become frustrated and lose motivation.

Relevant – Your goal should be relevant to whatever you are trying to achieve.

Timely – Objectives should have a completion date. Set a timeframe for your goal for next week, in three months, by next year. Having a completion point for your goal motivates you and provides you with a clear target to aim for.

Application Activity

Identify three to four work goals that you want to achieve in the next week, month, or year. Write them as SMART goals.

1.

2.

3.

4.

Setting Priorities

In today's work world we all have more things to do than we have time in which to do them. In addition, we don't have the energy, or resources to do everything equally well. No matter how hard we try we will not be able to complete everything.

The secret is to focus on those activities that give us the greatest return on our time investment. This is where prioritization is so helpful. When you prioritize you identify what goals, objectives and tasks are most important. Then give the high priority ones more of your attention, energy, and time.

Let's now focus on how to prioritize. Begin by learning to identify your ABC's. Alan Lakein, the renowned time management guru, developed this system.[97]

A - priorities are the most important – start with these first

B - priorities are the next most important

C - priorities are the least important – try to spend as little time as possible on these

Application Activity

1. Go back to the goals that you developed in the goal setting activity and prioritize them.

2. Assign either an A, B or C to them based on their importance.

Write a daily "To Do" list

The final time management technique that we will look at is to write a daily "To Do" list.[98] If you don't already do this, it is a straightforward technique that can increase your productivity by up to 25 percent. Not only does it ensure that you don't forget anything, but it also saves you energy and stress.

Let's look at when you should develop a "To Do" list. Some people find it useful to take 5-10 minutes at the beginning of each day to develop their list. Others find it best to develop their list the day before. They complete it before they leave work or before they go to bed because it clears their mind and enables them to relax.

It is also important to write down your tasks rather than keep them in your head. Some people prefer writing them on a piece of paper, while others like to use their computer, BlackBerry®, or other device. It is best to experiment to find out what works for you.

After you've listed all your tasks, review your "To Do" list and decide on the priority for each task.

There are four steps to creating a "To Do" list

Step 1: Create a list of tasks

Focus on what you need to do. Keep your list at a manageable length.

Step 2: Assign each task a priority

Use the priority system we discussed earlier:

Tasks that most important are "A" tasks. They have the highest priority. Focus on these tasks first.

Tasks that are next most important are "B" tasks. They rank second.

The least most important tasks are "C" tasks and rank third.

Step 3: Estimate the time involved

Once you have created and ranked the list, estimate the amount of time it will take to complete the task. This might be difficult at first but as you gain experience through practice your accuracy will improve.

Step 4: Update your "To Do" list

Review you list of tasks on an ongoing basis and keep it up-to-date. You may need to reassign priorities and completion time frames.

Application Activity

1. Write a "To Do" list using the form provided for you

2. Allocate priorities using the A, B, C system

3. In the space provided estimate the amount of time each task will take

To Do List

Date: _____

Task	Priority (A,B,C)	Estimated Time
1.		
2.		
3.		
4.		
5.		
6.		
7.		
8.		
9.		

10.		
11.		
12.		

Planning and Organizing

Whenever we have a major objective (or, as we will refer to it, a project) to achieve, we need to plan and organize. First, we must determine "What are we are going to do?" Then we must plan "How are we going to do it?" From there we organize the resources or "Who will be involved?" the time it will take or "When will it be done?" and the money needed or "How much will it cost?" to accomplish each step. The diagram below depicts how these questions are like the pieces of a puzzle and when they all fit together neatly we have a good plan.

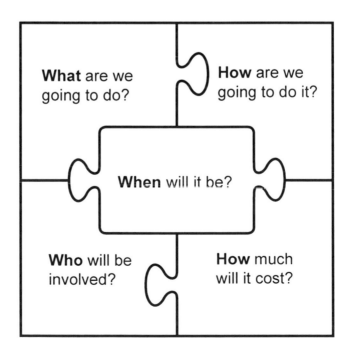

The more time and energy we put into answering these questions the less likely we, our department, team, or project, will go off track. Let's look at each piece of the puzzle individually.

What are we going to do?

At this stage, we define our objective or goal. A major part of this is defining the scope or the major project deliverable(s). When defining the scope it is just as important to define what is outside of the scope as what is inside. By doing this we help to manage the expectations for the project. We also need to determine how we will know when the project is complete and if it was a success or not. The completion criteria will state what has to be in place or happen for the project to be considered complete. The criteria for success will be a way of measuring whether or not the project achieved its goals. Finally, we should include how much money we will have to spend on the project because, generally, the budget is assigned to us up front and we need to figure out how to work within it.

Remember to keep the **SMART** acronym in mind when developing objectives or goals.

An example of a **SMART** objective or goal is: *"The purchasing team's Holiday Lunch will be held on December 3rd and only the purchasing team members will attend. 90% of the team members must rate the lunch as enjoyable or better and it will cost no more that $15 per person."*

If we break this example down, we can see:

- **Scope** – the Holiday Lunch for the purchasing team and only the purchasing team

- **Completion Criteria** – will be held on December 3rd

- **Criteria for Success** – 90% of the team members rate the lunch as enjoyable or better

- **Budget** – will cost no more than $15 per person

How are we going to do it?

In answering this question, we determine how we are going to achieve the objective or execute the project. This is comprised of two parts. First, how will we control the project as it progresses. Second, how we will break down the work. In terms of how we will control the project, we need to answer the following questions:

- How will the progress of time, cost, and resources be monitored?
- How will quality be assured?
- How will changes to the scope be controlled?
- How will issues be managed?
- How will risk be managed?

Then we need to create a work breakdown by breaking the work down into small, manageable pieces. First, we would normally break the project down into phases or fairly large chunks, for example, if we were building a cottage the phases might be:

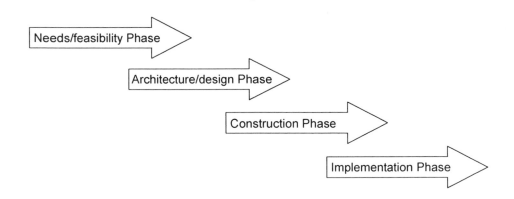

You will notice that the phases do overlap to some extent because we are frequently able to start one phase before we have completely finished the previous one.

Once our phases are in place we need to break the work down further into activities. Each activity will have a deliverable at the end of it or something tangible that will be accomplished by the activity. These deliverables become the milestones by which we measure the progress of the project. For example, if we take the construction phase, this could be broken down into activities, such as; pour the foundation, build the first floor, build the second floor, put on the roof. For the pour the foundation activity, our deliverable could be a completed foundation ready to support the building of the first floor. This activity would need to be broken down into a series of tasks necessary to complete the activity or deliverable. The tasks for this activity would be: dig the hole for the foundation, put the forms in place, mix the concrete, pour the concrete, pour the floor, and remove the forms. These tasks become our small manageable pieces. Once all of the tasks are completed, we will have the deliverable of a complete foundation and know that we have completed the pour the foundation activity.

Example of the Work Breakdown

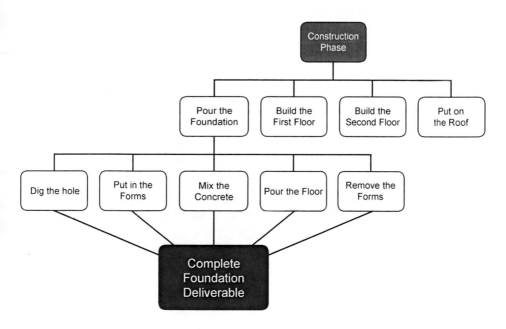

Who will be involved?

To answer the above question we need to answer the following questions:

- Who will experience an impact?
- What roles & responsibilities do the deliverables demand?
- What team structure is needed?

When determining who will experience an impact, we need to look at which areas will be involved during the project, which areas will be affected by the results of the project, if necessary who will provide the strategic guidance for the project, and whether external supplies need to be involved. Once we know who will experience an impact, we then need to determine the roles and responsibilities necessary to create the deliverables. By clearly defining the roles and responsibilities, we lessen confusion over assignments. Finally, we must determine the team structure. Depending on the size of the project, the team could be comprised of one person for a small project, or for a very large project, it could be made up of a Project Manager, multiple team leaders, and many team members.

When will it be done?

For this piece of the puzzle we look at how we arrive at our schedule for when the project will be done. To determine this we make use of the work breakdown, and the people that we have decided we need. Once you have completed the work breakdown the next steps to create a schedule are:

1. Examine task dependencies, or determine what tasks need to be completed before other tasks can be started, and what tasks can be done simultaneously.

2. Apply estimates of effort, or how long we think it would take for one person to complete each task.

3. Determine the critical path; this is the longest path in our schedule with no slack time. Tasks on this path affect the project end date. If a task on this path takes longer than expected the project completion date will be delayed. We may have multiple paths on our schedule as certain tasks can be done simultaneously but the critical path is the most important one.

4. Add resources to reduce the critical path. Sometimes you are able to reduce the time a task takes by adding additional resources. For example, if you were driving from Toronto to Florida (about a 24 hour drive), you can reduce the time by adding additional drivers as one or two drivers can sleep while

the other drives. This eliminates the need for rest breaks during the trip. However, sometimes adding additional resources cannot reduce the time a task takes. For example, if you are driving a truck from Toronto to Kingston (about a 3 hour drive) you cannot reduce the time it takes to get there by adding more drivers.

5. Check resource usage. You must check to make sure you have not over booked any of the people on the project (be sure to check for any commitments they may have to other projects when doing this). You cannot have any one person performing more than one task at a time.

At the end of this stage you will have a schedule that states all the tasks that need to be accomplished, the order they must be accomplished in, how long and how many people each task will take. It will culminate in a date when the project will be finished.

How much will it cost?

The final piece of the puzzle is "How much will it cost?" Here we look at the project costs over the duration of the project and beyond. Projects today are most often allotted a specific amount of money to spend. When answering this question we are really determining how we will spend that money and whether it makes sense to spend the money in this manner. One way to do this is to perform a cost-benefit analysis looking at how much each task in the project is going to cost and determine if the benefits, either tangible or intangible, outweigh the costs associated with the project. If the benefits don't outweigh the costs then it does not make sense to continue.

Once we have answered all these questions and the puzzle pieces fit neatly together we have a well organized plan regarding how we will achieve the objective or execute the project.

Application Activity

Think about a major objective or project you want/need to achieve. Then answer the questions below to plan and organize how you will achieve it:

1. What are we going to do?

2. How are we going to do it?

3. Who will be involved?

4. When it be completed by?

5. How much will it cost?

Maintaining High Standards for Themselves and Others

In this section, we will talk about the abilities that Organized Golds have regarding setting and maintaining standards.   They set high standards for themselves and others, they use their attention to detail to identify and correct mistakes, and they are willing and able to give others feedback to correct errors.

Setting Standards

A performance standard describes the level of performance that is acceptable or not acceptable. What distinguishes Organized Golds is that they are not only focused on meeting these standards but also exceeding them. For example, a typical standard might be to process 20 new applications per day.   An Organized Gold would probably try to exceed that number and find ways to improve the process so that 25 applications are processed each day.

It is important to set performance standards because it clarifies what is required for performance and acts to motivate us to achieve high standards. When setting performance standards these questions can be useful:

- What does an acceptable level of performance look like?
- How many or how much is needed to meet performance expectations?

- How long should it take to perform this job?

- What behaviours are required in your work area to promote teamwork, leadership, creativity, customer service?

- What results would meet/exceed the standard?

- What is the difference between good and poor performance?

Application Activity

1. Write down a task that you or another person needs to perform.

2. What does an acceptable level of performance look like?

3. What level of performance would exceed performance expectations?

Attention to Detail

Another area where Organized Golds excel is attention to detail. Because of their high standards they strive for perfection. To be detail-oriented means paying attention, noticing details and caring about them. Along with a detail-orientation comes the ability to notice and correct mistakes. For example, when proofreading documents they will pick out all of the small mistakes that others might miss.

Giving Others Feedback for Improvement

Once Organized Golds have found mistakes in their own work they will correct it. Equally, if they find mistakes in other's work they will let that person know about it. They usually do this with a genuine desire for performance improvement.

When giving feedback to others it is important to do it in a constructive manner – one in which the other person feels helped and not criticized. Feedback helps keep behaviour on target and thus better achieve important goals. When giving feedback there are three parts you should think through – the timing, the person's behaviour, and the consequences of their behaviour.

Timing

- The timing should be appropriate. In general, give feedback as soon as possible after noticing the mistake. However, other factors such as the person's readiness to receive feedback, or lack of privacy should be considered.

Behaviour

- Be specific – don't generalize. It is important to describe the person's behaviour as specifically and accurately as possible[99] Rather than saying "You made several errors," it would be more appropriate to say, "You did not include page numbers and I noticed that you spelled some of the team members' names incorrectly."

- Describe the person's behaviour don't attack or evaluate it. Avoid judging the person by making comments like "You are inconsiderate." Rather state the person's behaviour, for example, "In the meeting yesterday you interrupted me twice before I could finish my idea." This reduces the need for the individual to react defensively.

- Sometimes it is appropriate to indicate how you feel when the person exhibits the behaviour that you want to change. Some Temperaments will feel comfortable indicating their feelings and others will not. Equally, some Temperaments will be swayed by emotion and others will not find it important. If you decide to share your emotions, it is important to avoid falling into the trap of saying "You made me feel angry." Own up to your feelings by saying, "I felt angry." This kind of statement is less likely to illicit a negative reaction from the other person.

Consequences of Behaviour

- People need to have a reason to change. You can motivate changes by explaining how the behaviour affects you negatively. You need to spell out the concrete or tangible effects of the behaviour on you.[100] These consequences generally fall into the category of causing you extra work, wasting your time, interfering with your ability to do your job, harming your belongings, or costing you money. Therefore, for example, you might say, "When you keep asking me questions about my social life I get behind in completing my work." This explains the impact on you when the person acts in that way.

Application Activity

Think of somebody that you need to give feedback to and write a feedback statement. Then review it to ensure that it meets the feedback criteria we have outlined.

Maintaining Corporate Culture

When referring to corporate culture we are really talking about the organization's values, customs, traditions, and meanings that make a company unique. Some say corporate culture is the character of an organization because it symbolizes the vision of the company's founders. Organized Golds who have been with an organization for a long period can often help keep an organization grounded, especially in times of change. They do this by upholding and sharing the organization's values, customs, traditions, and meanings and maintaining the status quo. The Organized Golds truly believe in the old saying "if it ain't broke don't fix it."

In times of change, Organized Golds share their experiences about what has been tried in the past and what worked, and they work to preserve what is currently working well. Because of their strong sense of tradition they often know and are able to explain the history behind why an organization is the way it is. They know and are willing to share the reasons why certain structures, roles, rules, procedures, and policies exist. By learning about and respecting these past experiences and history we can greatly enhance how effectively organizational change is implemented. Often we are able to avoid repeating mistakes that were made in the past by taking this information into account when planning and implementing any kind of change. Some key questions a company/organization should ask prior to implementing change are:

1. What is the relevant history behind why our organization is the way it is?

2. What are the reasons for the structure, roles, rules, policies, and procedures we have in place today?

3. Do those reasons still hold true and make sense for the company/ organization today?

4. If they don't, which of them should we look at changing or eliminating?

5. What, if anything, is wrong with what we are currently doing?

6. Why change if what we are currently doing is working?

7. Is there any evidence that this change will improve the situation?

8. Has the proposed change ever been tried by anyone before?

9. When, where, why, and how will the change be implemented?

10. Once all of these questions have been satisfactorily answered most Organized Golds will be willing to work to help move any change ahead while still maintaining the traditions and status quos that make sense for the organization.

Application Activity

Think about a change that has been proposed within your own organization, it could be either a small or a large change, and answer the questions below. You may need to do some research about your organization's corporate culture to answer them effectively. Once you have determined answers to all of the questions think about which of the corporate traditions and status quo still make sense to maintain and how you can go about supporting the change.

1. What is the relevant history behind why our organization is the way it is?

2. What are the reasons for the structure, roles, rules, policies, and procedures we have in place today?

3. Do those reasons still hold true and make sense for the organization today?

4. If they don't still hold true which of them should we look at changing or eliminating?

5. What, if anything, is wrong with what we are currently doing?

6. Why make changes if what we are currently doing is working?

7. Is there any evidence that this change will improve the situation?

8. Has the proposed change ever been tried by anyone before?

9. When, where, why, and how will the change be implemented?

15

Abilities Associated with Authentic Blues

As we have seen earlier in the book Authentic Blues have many abilities. Four of these abilities are:

- Listening, understanding the other's perspective, and empathizing with them.

- Motivating, inspiring, and encouraging others.

- Bringing a creative and intuitive lens to the problem solving process.

- Acting in an authentic manner.

Listening and Empathizing with Others

According to various experts we can spend up to 50% of our time listening – yet many of us do not listen as well as we could. There are two main sets of skills associated with listening: non-verbal and verbal listening skills.

Non-verbal Listening Skills

Non-verbal listening skills refer to how we physically demonstrate that we are listening. Facing the speaker squarely helps communicate our involvement.[101] It is also important to maintain an open position with arms and legs uncrossed if we cross our arms or legs we can be seen as defensive or closed. Good listeners lean slightly towards the speaker as this communicates interest in what the speaker is saying. Effective eye contact also demonstrates our attentiveness to the other person. We demonstrate that we are listening when we focus our eyes softly on the speaker and occasionally look away. Too much eye contact or staring is seen as unfriendly while too little can indicate disinterest. Good listeners position themselves at an appropriate distance to the speaker. Too much distance indicates a lack of connection while too little distance tends to raise the speaker's anxiety.

Application Activity

Have a conversation with a trusted colleague or friend who is willing to give you feedback. Prior to the feedback conversation, give them the following Non-verbal Listening Skills Checklist and ask them to have a conversation with you and then give you feedback on your non-verbal skills. Once you have received their feedback, identify the areas where you should improve. Over the next week make an effort to practice incorporating these changes into your conversations. At the end of the week have another conversation with the same person. Ask them to give you feedback using the same checklist to see how much improvement you have made.

Non-verbal Listening Skills Checklist

- ❏ Face the speaker squarely
- ❏ Maintain an open posture with arms and legs uncrossed
- ❏ Lean slightly forward in the direction of the speaker
- ❏ Maintain soft eye contact
- ❏ Position yourself at an appropriate distance to the speaker

Verbal Listening Skills

Restatement

When we restate we summarize the essence of the other person's content in our own words. It shows that we are listening intently, clarifies the sender's real message, and helps us to truly understand the message. A good restatement is:

- Concise;
- A summary of only the essence of the speaker's message;
- Focused solely on the content of the speaker's words; and
- Stated in the listener's, not the speaker's own words.

Restatement can begin with a phrase like:

- *"If I understand what you are saying..."*
- *"What you're saying is..."*
- *"To summarize what you have said..."*

Reflection of Feelings

The reflection of feelings involves mirroring back to the speaker, in a precise way, the emotions that we believe the speaker is experiencing. This demonstrates that you understand, recognizes the non-verbal messages, and helps to calm the speaker down. In order to become more aware of the speaker's feelings:

- Make note of any feeling words the speaker uses;
- Pay attention to the general content of the message;
- Observe the person's body language; and
- Ask yourself, "If I were having this experience, what would my feelings be?"

A reflection statement might sound like:

- *"That must have been annoying"* or
- *"I can appreciate that you felt sad".*

Application Activity

After each speaker's comment please write an appropriate restatement or reflection statement. Share your responses with another person and ask them for feedback on whether you used restatement or reflection appropriately.

1. **Speaker**: I am at the end of my rope! Every time I complete work for my team leader she finds something wrong with it. She does not seem to approve of anything I do and it is really beginning to bother me.

Listener:

2. **Speaker:** I am having sleepless nights about what to do about the new position that I have been offered at work. I do want to get ahead but this position will require a lot of overtime. My children are still small and I want to spend as much time as possible with them.

Listener:

3. **Speaker:** I hate two-faced people. When I told Jane I could not meet the deadline, she said that it was OK to my face. Then she complained behind my back to everyone else at work. I do not like working with hypocritical people.

Listener:

4. **Speaker:** When Dragan got sick and was off for several weeks the whole team pitched in to get the job done. It is the best team experience I have ever had. People came in early and left late just to make sure that our deadlines were met.

Listener:

Empathy

Empathy is very closely aligned to effective listening and it is the ability to put yourself in the other person's shoes and see the world as that person sees it. In his book *People Skills*, Robert Bolton indicates that the best way to understand empathy is to see it on a continuum between apathy and sympathy.[102]

Apathy	Empathy	Sympathy
"Who cares!"	"You seem very upset today"	"That is just so awful"
"Not my problem"	"Sounds like that really took it out of you"	"I feel terrible for you"

When someone is apathetic they choose not to become involved and they demonstrate a lack of interest or concern for the other person and their situation. Both verbally and non-verbally, they send a message that they don't want to know about or become part of the other person's problem. Sometimes we need to be apathetic – it is important for our own sense of self-preservation that we do not get involved in every problem.

At the other end of the continuum is sympathy. According to Bolton, we demonstrate sympathy when we "feel for" a person while empathy is "feeling with" the other. With sympathy there is a danger of becoming over involved with the other person. Rather than helping them deal with the issue a sympathetic response may result in them becoming more bogged down and depressed by their problem.

An empathetic person on the other hand has the ability to sense the other persons feeling of love, anger, hate, joy, distress, and/or anxiety without taking on the same feeling because they are able to maintain a degree of detachment. There are three skills sets involved with empathy:

1. Truly understanding how the other person is feeling while still maintaining objectivity.

2. Taking the time to understand what caused or ignited the feeling.

3. Sharing your perceptions of what is happen with the other person in such a way they feel heard and understood.

Application Activity

Please read the following situation and answer the questions below based the previous descriptions.

Situation

One of your co-workers has just received a phone call telling them that a close friend from childhood has committed suicide. As they explain their situation to you they become tearful and their voice is shaky.

Questions

1.   What would be an apathetic response in this situation?

2.   What would be a sympathetic response in this situation?

3.   What would be an empathetic response in this situation?

Motivating and Encouraging Others

Many Authentic Blues believe in human potential and the cultivation of life long learning. They are willing to take the time and energy to help others develop their own potential. One of the ways they do this is by engaging in growth conversation to help others. Once they have initiated the conversation they will ask powerful questions, listen empathetically, and help the person think of potential options for growth. As soon as the person has determined a course of action, Authentic Blues will give them ongoing support as they change and grow.

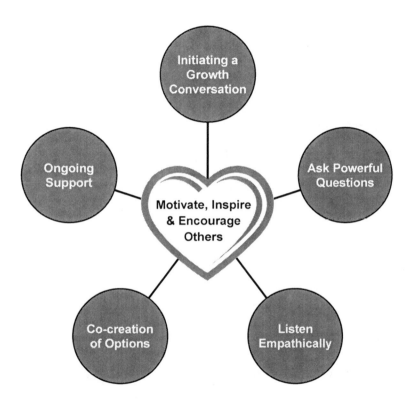

Initiating the Growth Conversation

Whether in a formal helping role (counsellor or coach) or an informal one (a friend), helpers will look for opportunities to initiate a growth conversation with others. In a more formal role they may help the client/employee identify their goals for this type of conversation. In an informal situation helpers can often sense when someone is struggling and looking for new direction and they will initiate a conversation with them.

Ask Powerful Questions

When it comes to understanding the situation and the other person's perspective, helpers ask powerful questions. Some questions that can be useful are:

- What is currently happening in more detail?

- What is really the issue here, the sticking point?

- What action have you taken so far?

- What obstacles do you need to overcome on the way?

- What resources do you already have? (skill, time, enthusiasm, money, support)

- What option can you think of regarding how to handle this situation?

- What other resources will you need? Where will you get them from?

- When were you able to handle this situation in the past? How did you handle it?

Listen Empathetically

Empathetic listeners can often see the deeper layers in what others are saying. This is because they are not only attuned to the words that a person is using, but also their body language, facial expression, and tone of voice. Others really feel heard and understood. Empathetic listeners will often have intuitive insights that they are willing to share and this can often lead to powerful learning on the part of the other person.

Co-creation of Options

The next step in the process is to co-brainstorm potential options to help the other person move forward. This requires the use of creative and intuitive thinking to come up with unique options for the other person to consider.

Once the list has been developed the next step is to mutually examine each of the options to determine which will best resolve the current situation.

Ongoing Support

Another helping technique is to give on-going support to the individual as they grow and change. This may involve having another growth conversation again if the person faces obstacles or it may involve reinforcing positive changes as they occur. One of the best ways to reinforce positive change is to give positive feedback. The following guidelines are useful:

1. Be specific when you give positive feedback. If the positive feedback is too global, for example, "you are a wonderful report writer," people don't tend to believe it. If you describe exactly what you appreciate it is easier for the other person to take it in and continue that type of behaviour, for example, "You wrote a concise report that focused on the most important points."

2. Praise progress towards a goal. Do not wait until the person is doing the task perfectly. Give feedback when the person is proceeding in the right direction as this can be very motivating.

3. Only give positive feedback when you sincerely mean it. People instantly know if you are being insincere and they may feel manipulated.

4. Choose your time and place. Give positive feedback as soon as possible after you observe the behaviour. Consider whether the person should receive feedback from you in private or in front of others.

Application Activity

Think of someone who would be receptive to helping you enhance your skills as a growth facilitator. Working with that person:

1. Plan how you would initiate a growth conversation with them.

2. What powerful questions would you ask?

3. Reflecting on the listening activity you did earlier in this chapter how would you demonstrate that you are listening empathically?

4. How will you co-create options with them?

5. What might you do to give support on an on-going basis?

Being Intuitive

Have you ever been driving somewhere for the first time and when you come to a fork in the road you instinctively (and correctly) turn left without looking at the map because you know that is the right way to go? Or have you ever been talking to a friend and know that something is wrong in their life and when you ask them you find out you were right? Another experience that you may have had is working on a problem at work and out of the blue you know how to resolve the situation. You know that you are right even though you don't know where the answer came from. These are all examples of how intuition might work. Most of us have had these intuitive flashes but choose to ignore them because we don't trust them, don't understand them, or don't consider them logical. We therefore miss out on an important source of information and insight for ourselves.

The Oxford English Dictionary defines "Intuition" as the "ability to understand or know something immediately, without conscious reasoning."[103] It is derived from the Latin word "intueri" which means "to see within." It is a way of knowing, of sensing the truth without explanations. Perhaps one of the best ways to look at intuition is to see it as a form of intelligence just as we would regard musical or spatial intelligence as a different form of intelligence.

There are many benefits to becoming intuitive. One of the major benefits is that it promotes effective communication because it can make us more sensitive to the people around us and help us not to hurt those that are important to us.

Intuition can also lead to greater creativity because it allows us to see possibilities that others cannot.

How to Activate and Use your Intuition

1. The first step is to be aware of when you are having an intuitive moment. Some of us just have a sense of knowing, while others may get a physical sensation or even experience an awareness around or above them. Some people indicate it comes in the form of a premonition or picture while others say that it comes to them in the form of words or thoughts.

2. Once we have had an intuitive flash the next step is to treat it as a valid source of information. At this point many of us discount it as illogical or irrational and do not use the information in any way. While we are not recommending that you make a major decision based solely on your intuition, we suggest that once you receive an intuitive insight you check it out by gathering more information or talking to others.

3. When sharing your intuition with others there are a number of phrases that can be useful:

"I have a hunch that…"

"I have a sense that…"

"Can I share something with you?"

"Does this make any sense to you?"

Application Activity

To allow you to tap into your intuition:

1. Book an appointment in your calendar each day for the next two weeks when you can spend some uninterrupted time alone.

2. Find a place where you can be comfortable and free of distractions.

3. Start by breathing gently in through your nose and out through your mouth. While doing this observe the process of breathing.

4. Be sensitive to any hunches, "gut feelings", or intuitions you might get. It may come to you in many forms like a premonition, words, thoughts, or just a sense of knowing. Don't discount anything that comes to you – let it flow.

5. Be patient. This is something that will take practice.

Being Authentic

As their name suggests authenticity is of upmost importance to many Authentic Blues. To be authentic basically boils down to living according to your values. Values are strongly held beliefs about what is good, right, and appropriate to the individual. They are deep-seated and remain constant over time. We accumulate our values from our experiences in childhood based on teachings and observations of our parents, teachers, religious leaders, and other influential and powerful people. An authentic person is someone who's values and actions are in alignment.

Let's look at an example of Jane, a customer service representative who tries to live an authentic life. Some of her main values are order, harmony, and integrity. She:

- Has a neat and tidy workspace and is able to put her hands on product and service information in order to answer customer's inquiries efficiently.

- Has a good working relationship with both her co-workers and management.

- Treats her clients with respect.

- Deals with a certain amount of sensitive or confidential information and ensures that that information is protected.

- At times, has to give clients unpleasant information and always does it in an honest but tactful manner.

There are advantages to being authentic. People tend to trust authentic people more because there is a congruence between who they are and what they do. Authentic people are more willing to accept constructive feedback and make changes. They are generally happier and usually have more energy.

Application Activity

Make a list of your core values.

Think about how you spend your time. Does it align with your core values?

If your actions do not align with your core values what changes can you make in your life to bring them into alignment or to live a more authentic life?

16

Conclusion

As you finish this book we hope that you have been engaged in a process of self discovery and learning. Our goal was for you to come away with a better understanding of yourself, be proud of the strengths that you bring to any situation, and aware of the challenges that you may want to work on. We also hope you have an increased tolerance for those whose temperament is different from your own. As Scott Campbell said in the Forward:

> "Now I am better able to realize that the other person is not intentionally trying to frustrate me, hurt me, or be difficult. They are just being their temperament. Realizing this makes interactions much more effective, far less frustrating, and way more fun".

People with different temperaments bring different gifts to the table and we all need to acknowledge and respect these. The information in this book should never be used to stereotype or label people but rather be used as a tool to help understand the unique differences that we all have. Additionally, we need to remember that we are all plaid - although we have a preferred temperament, we all, to a greater or lesser extent, use all of the temperaments.

In addition to an appreciation of Temperament, recognizing the difference between introversion and extraversion is very useful in understanding yourself and others. It is one of the main reasons we chose to work with Personality Dimensions® and use this approach to Temperament theory. Introversion and extraversion apply to all four Temperaments, so it is important to have an understanding of both because they play an important role in our interpersonal communications. Remember introverts do their best decision-making, thinking and learning when they have the time for quiet reflection and are able to work on their own. Extraverts on the other hand are at their best when they have the opportunity to interact with others, discuss their thoughts, and brainstorm new and creative ideas.

When we look at superstars like Pierre Elliot Trudeau or Martin Luther King we can observe the best that Inquiring Greens have to offer. As big picture conceptual thinkers they look at the overall situation, critically examine how it works and find ways to improve it. They are not scared to state what they think and they fight for what they believe is right even in the face of opposition. You only have to think about Martin Luther King to see how coolly and calmly Inquiring Greens generally present themselves – even in crises. As leaders, they can be effective change agents because they can envision a future strategic direction for their team, department or organization. The Inquiring Green employee flourishes in situations where they can use their big picture focus, logic, competence and knowledge to achieve goals. As leaders or employees, they are not always as comfortable as other temperaments when interacting with people. Others may see them as cold and aloof and at times Inquiring Greens can become impatient with people.

Resourceful Oranges such as Richard Branson or Celine Dion often command significant admiration from the rest of us because of their style and grace. They take pride in becoming skilled performers and work hard to perfect their technique in whatever interests them - it does not matter if it is an instrument, a tool, a sales pitch, an acting role, or a bulldozer. They are hands on practical people who use whatever is at hand to achieve their goals. Of all the styles, they are the most adaptable, often being referred to as chameleons, and this is a huge asset in the work force of today where change is constant. And last but not least they take a light-hearted attitude towards life and the other temperaments benefit from their sense of fun and playfulness. As leaders, they are action oriented, practical, tactically gifted, and masters at taking charge in crisis situations. Resourceful Orange employees come into their own in work environments where they can work hard to achieve their goals without unnecessary constraints. If they do feel constrained or bored they may have a tendency to rebel or act out. Also, Resourceful Oranges are true risk takers and sometimes they can get themselves into potentially challenging or dangerous situations at work, home, or in the world at large.

What would society do without the Organized Golds? We only need to look at Queen Elisabeth II or Wayne Gretsky to see how dependable and reliable they are and how effectively they uphold the traditions of the society in which they live. Many of us rely on their ability to prioritize, plan, and organize their work, families, and the communities in which they live. They help us to achieve the best results by setting high standards for themselves and those around them. Their common sense practical approach to life is an asset to those that need help being grounded in reality. The Organized Gold leader's supreme strength is in ensuring that the organization runs smoothly and efficiently by developing clear goals, setting priorities, and developing specific steps to achieve them. Unfortunately, Organized Golds can have a tendency towards anxiety because they often feel overly responsible for events. Their high standards can also cause others to perceive them as overly critical.

The Authentic Blues uphold society in a different way - of all the styles they are the most altruistic. They believe that happiness comes from helping others. And what better role models for Authentic Blues than Mother Theresa and Jimmy Carter. They excel in communicating with others because of their ability to listen to them, intuit what they are really saying and present their thoughts and feelings persuasively. Big picture thinkers, they enjoy dealing with conceptual data – especially when it relates to helping people.   They bring imagination and a creative flair to problem solving and situations which can be a great asset in a work environment. As leaders, their style is participative and they tend to develop a team-based environment where individuals work towards consensus on key issues. They often prefer leadership positions where they can be mentors, change agents, or advocates. Authentic Blues can have difficulty with conflict because they prefer to live and work in a harmonious environment. They can also be overly self critical and can sometimes take it too personally when receiving negative feedback from others.

We also wanted to leave you with the message that while we all have a preferred temperament, we always have the potential to tap into our non-preferred Temperament's associated skills and abilities and enhance our ability to use them. In chapters 12-15, we looked at some of the key skills associated with each temperament. For the Inquiring Greens we addressed some of the ways to look at situations from a large-scale systems perspective and how to be architects of change. We examined how to present themselves in a cool, calm, and collected manner and to bring a healthy scepticism to situations. With the Resourceful Oranges, we focused on their persuasion skills as well as how to take calculated risks based on a sound analysis of the situation. This temperament flourishes in new and crisis situations and we examined how to manage these situations effectively and how to keep an optimistic viewpoint throughout life. The Organized Golds truly live up to their name when it comes to organization. With this Temperament, we looked at ways to manage time by being goal oriented and developing a strong work ethic. Additionally, we focused on how to plan and organize and to set high standards for both ourselves and others. Finally, we looked at how to maintain corporate culture. The Authentic Blues approach life in a very authentic manner and they have a strong belief in human potential. For this temperament we focused on how to listen to others, understand their perspective, and empathize with them. We also focused on how to motivate, inspire, and encourage others and how to bring a creative and intuitive lens to the problem solving process.

Now that we have concluded our discussion on Temperament we wish you luck as you continue on your journey of self discovery and life long learning. In the Resources section, we have identified books and articles for future reading. If you would like to learn more about us, or the services we offer please visit our website at www.coloursavvy. com. If you would like to learn more about Personality Dimensions®, check out the "About PD" section on our web site, or visit www. personalitydimensions.com. We look forward to hearing from you and helping you continue on your journey of self-discovery.

Resources

In this section we have identified the resources we used and have given suggestions for further reading.

Chapter 1

[1] http://www.mindtools.com/CommSkll/CommunicationIntro.htm

[2] Keirsey, D. (1998). *Please Understand Me II*. Del Mar, CA: Prometheus Nemesis Book Company.
Please Understand Me II describes the four Temperaments and their relationships, parenting, leading, and intelligence. It contains in-depth descriptions of the four Temperaments that Keirsey named Rationals, Guardians, Idealists, and Artisans. This book has been identified as one of the leading works on personality theory.

[3] Don Lowry, a Californian school teacher, inspired by the work of Jung, Myers- Briggs, and Keirsey developed True Colors In 1979. It is a visual and highly interactive way to bring Temperament theory into the classroom. Using four colours, Green, Gold, Orange, and Blue he made the learning of personal preferences and individual similarities and differences fun and entertaining. For more information go to www.truecolors.org.

[4] Berens, L.V. (2006). *Understanding Yourself and Others: An Introduction To The 4 Temperaments*. Huntington Beach, CA: Telos Publications.
Inspired by the work of earlier theorists such as Myers- Briggs and Keirsey, Linda Berens provides a detailed analysis of the different aspects of Temperament such as core needs, values, talents and behaviors. She also defines the difference between our true self, our developed self and our contextual self.

[5] Maddron, T. (2002). *Living Your Colors: Practical Wisdom For Life, Love, Work, And Play*. New York, NY: Warner Books.
In simple, down-to-earth terms, Maddron describes the four Temperaments and their needs, learning styles, values, relationships, and personal troubles. Maddron refers to the 4 Temperaments as Blue, Orange, Gold, and Green.

[6] Personality Dimensions is a registered trademark of Career/LifeSkills Resources Inc. Personality Dimensions® is a Canadian tool developed by Career/Life Skills Resources Inc over a period of five years. The PD tool and approach relies heavily on the earlier theorists as will as independent studies. This tool adds a critical component of understanding ourselves and others – the preference for introversion or extraversion. They have also used descriptors that reflect important aspect of each Temperament – Inquiring Green, Organized Gold, Authentic Blue, and Resourceful Orange.

[7] Ibid.

Chapter 2

[8] Personality Dimensions is a registered trademark of Career/LifeSkills Resources Inc. The PD in Action booklet identified a number of needs of the Inquiring Green Temperament.

[9] Keirsey, D. (1998). *Please Understand Me II.*
Keirsey elaborates further on the Rationals in chapter 6: Rationals. We have referred to them as Inquiring Greens.

[10] Dunning, D. (2004). *Quick Guide To The Four Temperaments And Change: Strategies For Navigating Workplace Change.* Huntington Beach, CA: Telos Publications.
For those who want to read more about change and Temperament, this is an easy to use resource that looks at what organizations and individuals can do to make the change process easier for others. Dunning refers to the four Temperaments as Rational, Guardian, Idealist, and Artisan. We have used the terms Inquiring Green, Organized Gold, Authentic Blue, and Resourceful Orange.

[11] Keirsey, D. (1998). *Please Understand Me II.*

[12] Maddron, T. (2002). *Living Your Colors: Practical Wisdom For Life, Love, Work, and Play.*
In chapter 7: Troubles, Maddron describes the troubles and challenges of each of the four Temperaments.

[13] Keirsey, D. (1998). *Please Understand Me II.*
In chapter 9 on Leading and Intelligence Keirsey discusses the four Temperaments and their leadership characteristics.

[14] Maddron, T. (2002). *Living Your Colors: Practical Wisdom For Life, Love, Work, and Play.*
In chapter 10: the Workplace, Maddron discusses the Working Styles and leadership styles of the different Temperaments.

[15] Kalil, C. (1998). *Follow Your True Colors To The Work You Love.* Santa Ana, CA: True Colors, Inc. Publishing.

[16] http://en.wikipedia.org/wiki/Martin_Luther_King,_Jr
This site gives in-depth information on the life and achievements of Martin Luther King.

[17] http://en.wikipedia.org/wiki/Pierre_Trudeau
For more information on the life and achievements of Pierre Trudeau, this article is very useful.

[18] http://en.wikipedia.org/wiki/Woody_Allen
This site gives in-depth information on the life and achievements of Woody Allen.

Chapter 3

[19] Keirsey, D. (1998). *Please Understand Me II.*
David Keirsey elaborates further on Artisans in Chapter 3: Artisans. We refer to this Temperament as Resourceful Orange.

[20] Maddron, T. (2002). *Living Your Colors: Practical Wisdom For Life, Love, Work, and Play.*

[21] Ibid.
Chapter 5: Orange and Chapter 7: Troubles give more information on challenges for the Resourceful Orange.

[22] Keirsey, D. (1998). *Please Understand Me II.*
To read more about the leadership qualities of this Temperament, read about the tactical leader in Chapter 9: Leading and Intelligence.

[23] Maddron, T. (2002). *Living Your Colors: Practical Wisdom For Life, Love, Work, and Play.*
Maddron talks about the leadership qualities of this Temperament in Chapter 10: The Workplace.

[24] Ibid.
Maddron talks about working styles in Chapter 10: The Workplace.

[25] http://en.wikipedia.org/wiki/Ronald_Reagan
For more information on the life and achievements of Ronald Regan.

[26] http://www.woopidoo.com/biography/richard_branson.htm
For more information on the life and achievements of Richard Branson.

[27] http://en.wikipedia.org/wiki/Celine_Dion
For more information on the life and achievements of Céline Dion.

Chapter 4

[28] Personality Dimensions is a registered trademark of Career/LifeSkills Resources Inc. The *PD in Action* booklet identified a number of values and needs of the Organized Gold Temperament.

[29] Keirsey, D. (1998). *Please Understand Me II.*
David Keirsey elaborates further on Guardians in Chapter 4: Guardians which we refer to as Organized Golds.

[30] Maddron, T. (2002). *Living Your Colors: Practical Wisdom For Life, Love, Work, and Play.*
In Chapter 7: Troubles, Maddron describes the troubles and challenges of each of the four Temperaments.

[31] http://en.wikipedia.org/wiki/Elizabeth_II_of_the_United_Kingdom
This site gives in-depth information on the life and achievements of Queen Elizabeth II.

[32] http://en.wikipedia.org/wiki/Wayne_Gretzky
This site gives in-depth information on the life and achievements of Wayne Gretzky.

[33] http://en.wikipedia.org/wiki/Julia_Child
This site gives in-depth information on the life and achievements of Julia Child.

Chapter 5

[34] Segal, M. (2003). *Quick Guide To The Four Temperaments And Creativity.* Huntington Beach, CA: Telos Publications.

[35] Keirsey, D. (1998). *Please Understand Me II.*
Keirsey further elaborates on Idealists in Chapter 5. We refer to them as Authentic Blues.

[36] Ibid.
To read more about the leadership qualities of this Temperament, read about the diplomatic leader (Authentic Blue) in Chapter 9: Leading and Intelligence.

[37] Maddron, T. (2002). *Living Your Colors: Practical Wisdom For Life, Love, Work, and Play.* Maddron talks about the leadership qualities of this Temperament in Chapter 10: The Workplace.

[38] Dunning, D. (2004) *Quick Guide To The Four Temperaments And Change: Strategies for Navigating Workplace Change.* Huntington Beach, CA: Telos Publications.

[39] http://en.wikipedia.org/wiki/Oprah_Winfrey
To learn more about the life and times of Oprah Winfrey, go to this website.

[40] http://en.wikipedia.org/wiki/Mother_Teresa
To learn more about the life and times of Mother Teresa, go to this website.

[41] http://en.wikipedia.org/wiki/Jimmy_Carter
To learn more about the life and times of Jimmy Carter, go to this website.

Section 3

[42] Berens, L.V. (2006). *Understanding Yourself And Others: An Introduction To The 4 Temperaments.*
Berens has a section on stress and the different Temperaments where she refers to the four Temperaments as Stabilizer, Improviser, Catalyst, and Theorist. We use the terms Organized Gold, Resourceful Orange, Authentic Blue, Inquiring Green.

Chapter 6

[43] Martin, C. R., and Fields, M.U. (1998). Stress: How The Types Respond.
Gainesville, Fla.: Centre for Applications of Psychological Type.
For further reading, this is a great article on Stress and the Myers-Briggs Type. We have extracted information from the SJ, SP, NF, and NT for the Organized Gold, Resourceful Orange, Authentic Blue, and Inquiring Green.

[44] Maddron, T. (2002). *Living Your Colors: Practical Wisdom For Life, Love, Work, and Play.*

[45] Berens, L.V. (2006). *Understanding Yourself And Others: An Introduction To The 4 Temperaments.* Huntington Beach, CA: Telos Publications.

[46] Martin, C. R., and Fields, M.U. (1998). *Stress: How The Types Respond.*
The last page of this article identifies how the different Myers-Briggs Types behave when under stress.

[47] Maddron, T. (2002). *Living Your Colors: Practical Wisdom For Life, Love, Work, and Play.*
In the chapter on Troubles, Maddron explains how the other Temperaments can be useful when a person is stressed.

[48] Personality Dimensions is a registered trademark of Career/LifeSkills Resources Inc.

[49] Maddron, T. (2002). *Living Your Colors: Practical Wisdom For Life, Love, Work, and Play.*

[50] Kalil, C. (1998). *Follow Your True Colors To The Work You Love.*

[51] Maddron, T. (2002). *Living Your Colors: Practical Wisdom For Life, Love, Work, and Play.*

[52] Martin, C. R., and Fields, M.U. (1998). *Stress: How The Types Respond.*

[53] Maddron, T. (2002). *Living Your Colors: Practical Wisdom For Life, Love, Work, and Play.*

[54] Kalil, C. (1998). Follow Your True Colors To The Work You Love.

[55] Maddron, T. (2002). *Living Your Colors: Practical Wisdom For Life, Love, Work, and Play.*

Chapter 7

[56] Tieger, P., and Barron-Tieger, B. (1998). *The Art of Speed Reading People.* NY: Little, Brown and Company.
In Chapter 4, Paul Tieger and Barbara Barron-Tieger give invaluable insight into how to analyze the different Temperaments. They refer to the four Temperaments as Traditionalists, Experiencers, Conceptualizers, and Idealists. We use the terms Organized Gold, Resourceful Orange, Inquiring Green, Authentic Blue.

[57] Ibid.

[58] Personality Dimensions is a registered trademark of Career/LifeSkills Resources Inc.

[59] Tieger, P.D. and Barron-Tieger, B. (2001). *The Art of Speed Reading People.*

[60] Nash, S. (1999). *Turning Team Performance Inside Out: Team Types and Temperament for High-Impact Results.* Palo Alto, CA: Davis-Black Publishing

Chapter 8

[61] *Career Dimensions*™ ©2005 Career/LifeSkills Resources Inc.
Career/LifeSkills Resources has conducted extensive research on the jobs that appeal to each Temperament. Many of our listing of professions come from their research

[62] Tieger, P.D. and Barron-Tieger, B. (2001). *Do What You Are*. Boston, MA: Little, Brown and Company.
We summarized this information from the NT types in the book, which we refer to as Inquiring Greens.

[63] Ibid.

[64] Ibid.

[65] Ibid.

[66] Ibid.

[67] Ibid.

Chapter 9

[68] *Career Dimensions*™ ©2005 Career/LifeSkills Resources Inc.
Career/LifeSkills Resources has conducted extensive research on the jobs that appeal to each Temperament. Many of our listing of professions come from their research.

[69] Tieger, P.D. and Barron-Tieger, B. (2001). *Do What You Are*.
We summarized this information from the SP types in the book, which we refer to as Resourceful Oranges.

[70] Ibid.

[71] Ibid.

[72] Ibid.

Chapter 10

[73] *Career Dimensions*™ ©2005 Career/LifeSkills Resources Inc.
Career/LifeSkills Resources has conducted extensive research on the jobs that appeal to each Temperament. Many of our listing of professions come from their research.

[74] Tieger, P.D. and Barron-Tieger, B. (2001). *Do What You Are*.
We summarized this information from the SJ types in the book, which we refer to as Organized Golds.

[75] Ibid.

[76] Ibid.

[77] Ibid.

Chapter 11

[78] *Career Dimensions*™ ©2005 Career/LifeSkills Resources Inc.
Career/LifeSkills Resources has conducted extensive research on the jobs that appeal
to each Temperament. Many of our listing of professions come from their research.

[79] Tieger, P.D. and Barron-Tieger, B., (2001). *Do What You Are.*
We summarized this information from the NF types in the book, which we refer to as
Authentic Blue.

[80] Ibid.

[81] Ibid.

[81] Ibid.

Section 6

[82] Berens, L.V. (2006). *Understanding Yourself And Others: An Introduction To The 4
Temperaments.* Huntington Beach,
Berens has a section on stress and the different.

Chapter 12

[83] Senge, P., Roberts, C., Ross, R.B., Smith, B.J., And Kleiner, A. (1994). *The Fifth
Discipline Fieldbook: Strategies And Tools For Building A Learning Organization.* New
York, NY: Doubleday.

[84] Ibid.

[85] Senge, P., (1990). *The Fifth Discipline: The Art And Practice Of The Learning
Organization.* Doubleday: New York, NY.
Both books are useful if would like to read more about systems thinking.

[86] http://dictionary.sensagent.com/change+agent/en-en/

[87] Dunning. D (2004). *Quick Guide to the Four Temperaments and Change: Strategies
for Navigating Workplace Change.*

[88] Mehrabian, A. (1968). *Communication without words.* Psychology Today,
September 1968

[89] Bolton, R. (1979). *People Skills.* New York, NY: Simon & Schuster Inc.

Chapter 13

[90] Hankins, G. (2005). *The Power Of The Pitch: Transform Yourself Into a Persuasive Presenter and Win More Business.* Chicago, IL: Dearborn Trading Publishing.

[91] The article featuring David Cumberbatch first appeared in "Personnel Today Magazine", August 2006.

[92] http://www.livestrong.com/article/14727-becoming-a-risk-taker/.

[93] Hughes, M., Patterson, L.B. and Terrell, J.B. (2005) *Emotional Intelligence in Action: Training And Coaching Activities For Leaders and Managers.* San Francisco, CA.: Pfeiffer

[94] http://www.apahelpcenter.org/featuredtopics/feature.php?id=6&ch=1
Some of these ideas were adapted from the resilience section of this web site .For further reading, it has a comprehensive section on resilience.

[95] http://www.tirian.com/3d/d2/optimism.htm

Chapter 14

[96] Blanchard, K., Zigarmi, P. and Zigarmi, D., (1985). *Leadership And The One Minute Manager: Increasing Effectiveness Through Situational Leadership.* New York, NY: HarperCollins Publishers.
We adapted ideas from SMART for this section.

[97] Lakein, A. (1973). *How To Get Control Of Your Time And Your Life.* New York: Penguin Group.

[98] Ibid.

[99] Bolton, R., (1979). *People Skills: How To Assert Yourself, Listen To Others, and Resolve Conflict.*

[100] Ibid.

Chapter 15

[101] Bolton, R., (1979). *People Skills: How To Assert Yourself, Listen To Others, And Resolve Conflict.*

[102] Ibid.

[103] Thompson, D. (Ed.). (1993). *The Oxford Dictionary Of Current English.* (Second edition). Oxford: Oxford University Press.

CPSIA information can be obtained at www.ICGtesting.com
Printed in the USA
BVOW030833170212

283166BV00003B/1/P